What in the World is a Christian?

What in the World is a CHRISTIAN ?

John Blanchard

EVANGELICAL PRESS

EVANGELICAL PRESS
16/18 High Street, Welwyn, Hertfordshire AL6 9EQ, England.

© Evangelical Press 1982

First published 1975
First Evangelical Press edition 1982
Second impression 1984

ISBN 0 85234 167 9

Bible quotations are from the New International Version, unless
otherwise stated.

Typeset in Great Britain by Inset, Hertford Heath

Printed by Anchor Brendon Ltd., Tiptree, Colchester, England.

To Peter, Eric, Dave and Derek
with gratitude for your fellowship.

Contents

Introduction

'Who are *you*?'

The park-keeper's question cracked like a rifle-shot across Frankfurt's Tiergarten, jolting back to some kind of reality the ragged figure slouched untidily on a bench. Wearily, he raised his head, looked sadly at the official, and said, 'I wish to God I knew!'

Yet the speaker was no ordinary 'down-and-out', nor was he an uneducated moron. Arthur Schopenhauer, one of Germany's greatest philosophers, had spent years wrestling with the meaning of man's existence on the earth, but the sudden question had wrenched from him the terrible truth.

Schopenhauer's philosophy was essentially pessimistic. He taught that all existence is essentially evil — which goes a long way towards explaining both his identity crisis and his spiritual poverty. Even more tragic is the fact that many Christians are spiritually impoverished for a similar reason — their failure to understand and appreciate their true spiritual identity. This may be because of a lack of sound biblical teaching, or their own superficial approach to Scripture. It may follow frustratingly in the wake of their restless chasing after mystical 'experiences' or 'thrills', which leave them temporarily puffed up without being permanently built up. Whatever the reason, the result is always sub-normal Christianity.

I have long been convinced that there is no substitute for straightforward, biblical teaching in order to produce healthy, balanced and progressive Christians. Doctrine has a built-in dynamic to be found nowhere else. As Christ himself put it, 'The truth will set you free' (John 8:32). Basic biblical truth, clearly understood and resolutely applied, sets the Christian free from errors, excesses and eccentricities. Whether the issue is one of doctrine or practice, theology or morality, public worship or private living, the Christian's invariable starting-point should be 'What does the Scripture say?' (Romans 4:3.)

To come at the issue from another angle, too many Christians are suffering from homiletical shell-shock. They have been blasted and blistered, flogged and flayed, challenged and charged by one preacher after another to improve their spiritual standard of living, but often without a biblical explanation of what a Christian *already is.* Yet, surely, this is the only proper place to begin! To put it in a nutshell, the Bible's moral teaching amounts to this: *we are to become what we are.* It is my conviction that if Christians could get a firm grasp of this, then follow through its implications, their lives would be immeasurably enriched, and it is this conviction that led to the series of studies contained in this little book.

If you are looking for a detailed and scholarly exposition of Scripture, profound in depth and prophetic in element, then you have the wrong book! My aim has merely been to examine in a simple and straightforward way some of the words the Bible uses to describe a Christian, and then to apply their truth to everyday Christian living.

The outline of these chapters first took shape during the course of a flight across the United States, and the material in its original form was taught during a series of Bible Hours on summer houseparties held at Les Avants-sur-Montreux, Switzerland. Previous editions of the book have apparently been a great help to many Christians in various parts of the world, and I am grateful to John Rubens and Bill Clark of Evangelical Press for encouraging me to produce this revised version.

If this book helps you to be a wiser and better Christian, their efforts and mine will have been more than amply rewarded.

JOHN BLANCHARD

Banstead,
Surrey.
1982

1.

A Son
New birth, new life

1.

A Son
New birth, new life

With all due deference to storks and gooseberry bushes, we can state as a categorical fact that life begins with birth! And when all the miserable meanderings of modernists and others have been examined and rejected, we can state with equal certainty that spiritual life begins with spiritual birth. The clear, unequivocal teaching of Scripture is that unless a person has experienced this 'new birth' he has not even begun the Christian life. As Jesus said plainly to the religious leader Nicodemus, 'I tell you the truth, unless a man is born again, he cannot see the kingdom of God' (John 3:3). This means that a man does not become a Christian as a result of his upbringing, his moral effort, his religious affiliations, nor in any other way except by an experience so radical that Jesus called it being 'born again'.

This is confirmed by the way in which the Bible repeatedly describes a Christian as a child (or son) of God. In a brilliantly prophetic passage, God tells Hosea that believers will be called 'sons of the living God' (Hosea 1:10). The apostle Paul tells the Christians at Rome that 'Those who are led by the Spirit of God are sons of God' (Romans 8:14) and he encourages believers at Philippi to be 'blameless and pure, children of God without fault in a crooked and depraved generation' (Philippians 2:15). On another occasion, he writes to the Christians in Galatia and reminds them that as

believers they are 'all sons of God through faith in
Christ Jesus' (Galatians 3:26). The apostle John
rejoices in the same great truth and writes, 'How great
is the love the Father has lavished on us, that we
should be called children of God! And that is what we
are!' (1 John 3:1–2.)

What a stupendous truth this is! *Christians are not
merely followers; they are family members.* They have
the right to claim that astonishing relationship with the
sovereign and eternal God. Now, of course, there are
those who would say that this is overstating the case,
that no Christian has the *right* to claim such a thing,
that the best we can do is to try our best, and hope that
at the end of the day God will graciously receive us into
his family and kingdom. The answer to such an objec-
tion is to fall back right away on our overriding
principle — 'What does the Scripture say?'

In the opening chapter of John's Gospel, the writer
establishes the eternal deity of Christ, in telling us that
'The Word was God' (John 1:1). He then tells us of
Christ's coming into the world, of his rejection by the
world at large and by the Jewish people in particular.
Then he adds this: 'Yet to all who received him, to
those who believed in his name, he gave the *right* to
become children of God' (John 1:12). The Greek word
is *exousia,* and to illustrate its meaning we can look at
some other places where the same word is used. Speaking to the Jews at Jerusalem, Jesus said, 'For as the
Father has life in himself, so he has granted the Son to
have life in himself. And he has given him authority
(*exousia*) to judge because he is the Son of Man' (John
5:26–27). Jesus was not merely saying that he had the
moral muscle to pass judgement on men, overwhelming
them by some kind of force, but that he had the *right*
to do so. It was part of his office as the Son of Man.

Later, speaking about his own earthly life, he said,

'No one takes it from me, but I lay it down of my own accord. I have authority *(exousia)* to lay it down, and authority *(exousia)* to take it up again. This command I received from my Father' (John 10:18). As God, he acted with divine power; as man, he acted with delegated authority. Then, in the course of his amazing prayer recorded in John 17, Jesus reminds his heavenly Father that he had granted him 'authority *(exousia)* over all people that he might give eternal life to all those you have given him' (John 17:2). Again, the point of emphasis is not that of some kind of spiritual brute force, but rather of his divine right to rule in the affairs of men. Men could dispute it, but never deny it; it was his by divine right.

Now it is this same word, *exousia,* that John uses when he says that those who receive Christ, who believe in his name, are given 'the *right* to become children of God'. John is not saying that God gives us power to become children of God by ourselves, but rather that he has made us children of God by his own power, that he gives us his own authority to say that he has done so. There is a world of difference! What is more, *every* Christian has been given that authority. Young or old, weak or strong, mature or immature, every Christian is a child of God, and has been given divine authority to make that claim. That being so, it is nothing short of a tragedy that so many Christians seem to lack that settled, positive assurance, and appear to have no more than the courage of their confusions. Dr Billy Graham once said, 'Many Christians have settled down under their doubts as though they had contracted an incurable disease.' Yet when a Christian is in that state, his witness loses its cutting edge, the glow and warmth seep out of his worship, and he knows less and less of what Paul has in mind when he tells his readers, 'May the God of hope fill you with all joy and peace as you trust in him' (Romans 15:13).

For many people who are in that miserably unsatisfactory state I believe that the road to recovery begins by grasping hold of the tremendous truth that, regardless of their doubts and fears, God has given them the unalterable status of being members of his family, and as such has made them objects of his special and eternal love and care.

Having established that one basic fact, let us move on to look at three aspects of its truth. The first two are essentially doctrinal, and form the real heart of this particular study, while the third is practical, and points to the application of this truth in the Christian's life.

1. The mystery of being a son of God

Let us go back for a moment to the confrontation between Jesus and Nicodemus. After the religious leader's opening comment, Jesus got right to the heart of what he wanted to say: 'I tell you the truth, unless a man is born again, he cannot see the kingdom of God' (John 3:3). Apparently nonplussed by this amazing statement, Nicodemus asked, 'How can a man be born when he is old? Surely he cannot enter a second time into his mother's womb to be born!' (John 3:4.) Without examining the text further, it is obvious that Nicodemus had already missed the point. He was miles away from what Jesus was saying. In fact, the only other recorded words of Nicodemus in the whole dialogue were in the form of another question when, in reply to what Jesus told him about the working of the Holy Spirit in bringing a person into the kingdom of God, he asked, 'How can this be?' (John 3:9.)

Nicodemus had problems! He was completely out of his depth. He was thinking about physical life; Jesus was speaking about spiritual life. Jesus called him

'Israel's teacher' (John 3:10), but on this issue at least
he was not even in the kindergarten! Now, of course, as
Christians, we can look back at this incident and feel
that we are somewhat superior to Nicodemus. It is perfectly obvious to us that Jesus was speaking about a
spiritual birth and not a physical one. That is no mystery to us. Perhaps so, but there is something that at
this point needs to be underlined very carefully and
that is that although we do know the element of which
Jesus was speaking, we do *not* understand its essence.
After 2,000 years of exegesis and exposition, prising
and preaching, the new birth remains a complete
and utter mystery to us.

That is not always apparent in the Christian church
today. There is no denying that some forms of evangelism give the impression that all the mystery has been
evacuated from the new birth. It has been reduced to
a formula, a technique, a routine, a procedure. Without
wishing to be unkind, it seems as if for some it is a
matter of stand up, walk out, sign on, and you are in.
But that is both a travesty and a tragedy. To take away
the mystery from the new birth is to take away its
majesty — and the new birth is both mysterious and
majestic. The systems of men are no substitutes for the
sovereignty of God, and the church's heavy reliance on
them is undoubtedly a major reason for the vast number
of people who have at one time or another 'made a
decision', 'given their hearts to Jesus' or 'responded',
(some of the non-biblical terms used), but are now
wandering around in a spiritual wilderness. There is an
urgent need to recapture a biblical approach to the subject of the new birth, and we can at least begin to do so
by looking at two aspects of its essential mystery.
Firstly, its operation is mysterious. This comes out
clearly in what Jesus told Nicodemus: 'The wind blows
wherever it pleases. You hear its sound, but you cannot

tell where it comes from or where it is going. So it is with everyone born of the Spirit' (John 3:8). I had a remarkable experience of this during a convention at which I was preaching in Leptokarya in Northern Greece. A doctor friend of mine from Thessalonica had kindly invited me out to lunch with him and his family, and drove me a few miles down the coast to a delightful restaurant overlooking the sparkling Aegean Sea. As we went inside, it was a beautiful, still, warm day, with not a breath of wind. However, as we discussed the menu and prepared to order, I noticed the sky darkening and the curtains beginning to rustle in the wind. By the time we had ordered, a stiff wind was blowing and the first drops of rain began to fall. We were eventually served nearly two hours later — when the staff had mopped up the flooded kitchens, and cleared fallen trees from the car park! Yet by the time we finished our meal there was not a cloud in the sky and not a breath of wind! Where did the wind come from? Where did it go? We had no idea. It was a dramatic underlining of A.W. Pink's comment that 'The wind is irresponsible; that is to say, it is sovereign in its action.'

In the same way, the Holy Spirit moves like a mighty wind according to God's sovereign will, and no man can understand how or why he does so. Some years ago, I conducted a youth campaign in the town of Ballymoney, in Northern Ireland. When I arrived at Belfast Airport, I was met by one of the organizers and driven north into Co. Antrim. As we drove along, we found ourselves talking about the great days of revival in that part of the country. At one point he told me that we were then driving through an area where God had moved in a truly remarkable way, with many hundreds being converted. Suddenly, as we approached a major road junction, he said, 'You see these crossroads? The revival turned left there.' I thought I had misheard him, and told him

so, but he underlined what he was saying: 'From here
on, and right through the next town, the revival had no
effect at all, but immediately beyond the town, it broke
out again like a prairie fire, and swept all the way to the
coast.' I was speechless, struck dumb by an awesome
sense of the mysterious power of God. Here was something that man could neither organize nor explain. It
was God on the loose — mighty, marvellous, majestic
and mysterious!

'But', says somebody, 'that is revival with a capital
'R', something unique and that happens very seldom.
Surely the working of the Holy Spirit is not so mysterious in the case of every individual conversion?' Yes
it is! And that is precisely the point Jesus made to Nicodemus: 'So it is with *everyone* born of the Spirit.' Do
you find that a little difficult to believe? Then let me
ask you some questions. Can you tell me *how* you were
born again? You may be able to tell me the place, the
year, the month, the day, or even the time. You may be
able to tell me that it was under a certain man's ministry, or to give me the text of Scripture that gripped you.
But can you tell me *how* it happened? Can you tell me
how the Spirit of God opened your blind eyes, un-
stopped your deaf ears, pierced your darkened mind,
melted your hardened heart?

Let me take that a step further. If you were converted
at some kind of service or meeting, can you explain how
or why *you* were saved and other people in the same
gathering were completely untouched? The simple answer is that you cannot do so. The whole thing is a
mystery.

Secondly, the objects are mysterious. Now there are
some who might say that Christians are certainly mysterious objects, but that is not quite the point I want
to make here! Let me take you back to a statement we
noted earlier from one of John's letters: 'How great is

the love the Father has lavished on *us,* that *we* should be called children of God! And that is what we are!' (1 John 3:1.) Notice the words I have deliberately underlined. What staggers John is that God should have done such a thing to *us,* with all of our sin, rebellion, pride, impurity and selfishness! How amazing that in spite of our wretched and guilty state, God lavished his love upon us, drew us to himself, forgave our sin and honoured us with the title 'children of God'! As Isaac Watts put it,

Alas! And did my Saviour bleed?
And did my Sovereign die?
Would he devote that sacred head
For such a worm as I?

This is what I mean when I say that the objects of the new birth are mysterious. By any human reckoning or yardstick we would never give anything approaching that kind of honour to people such as we were. We choose the lovely and reject the unlovely, indulge the pleasant and ignore the unpleasant, but God does not work like that. As Paul says, 'God demonstrates his own love for us in this: *while we were still sinners,* Christ died for us' (Romans 5:8). When there was nothing good to be seen in us, and nothing good to be said for us, God loved us sufficiently to send his only, beloved Son into the world to save us, to bring us to himself. Charles H. Gabriel put his own sense of wonder like this:

I stand amazed in the presence
Of Jesus the Nazarene,
And wonder how he could love me,
A sinner, condemned, unclean.

But here is an even greater mystery. The Bible teaches that God set his saving love upon his people *even before they were born.* This is how Paul puts it: 'Praise be to the God and Father of our Lord Jesus Christ, who has blessed us in the heavenly realms with every spiritual blessing in Christ. For he chose us in him before the creation of the world to be holy and blameless in his sight' (Ephesians 1:3–4). The mystery deepens — and is utterly beyond any human explanation. God has loved us, chosen us, called us to himself, forgiven our sins and given us authority to be called his children, and no man living can understand, analyse or explain how or why he should do so. We can argue the niceties of theology until the proverbial cows come home, but ultimately we must reach a point where, in Charles Wesley's words, we are 'lost in wonder, love and praise', at the mystery of being a son of God!

2. The miracle of being a son of God

Becoming a son of God is not only a mystery, it is also a miracle. To illustrate this, let me take you back to the visit to Northern Ireland I mentioned a little earlier. When we reached Ballymoney, we began the final preparations for the youth campaign. My companion hired the Town Hall and got it ready for the informal coffee-bar approach we were using. Eventually, the meetings got under way, and God began to work in the hearts and lives of a number of the teens and twenties who came along. As the news began to filter through the town other, older people began to trickle in, perhaps largely out of curiosity. When I had finished speaking one night, one of the ministers organizing the campaign introduced me to two men from his congregation. They were apparently good-living, respectable men in the town — regular church-goers, too — but, as he told me bluntly in their presence, 'They are not saved, and they know it. You have a go at them!' It was all refreshingly frank, but more than a little embarrassing! However, we began to talk, and one of the men told me very honestly where he thought he stood spiritually. He was religious, a regular attender at church, a member of the choir. He read his Bible, he prayed, he tried to be an honest businessman and a good husband, but he knew he was not a Christian. Then came his summary: 'I know the gospel perfectly well, and all I need to do is to take one little step and I will become a Christian.' 'Sir,' I replied, 'you are not telling me the truth.' 'But I am,' he insisted, and then launched into a rerun of his spiritual pilgrimage, ending with his conviction that he only needed to take one little step and he would be saved. Again, I told him he was not telling me the truth, and again he told me the same story, ending in the same way. After deliberately letting this go on for some time, I turned to him and said, 'I don't doubt your life story, your attendance at church and so on, but the bit you have got wrong is over what it will take to make you a Christian. What you need is not a little thing, nor is it something you can do. What you need is a miracle — a miracle greater than the creation of the world.' He was flabbergasted, and very soon was arguing along the same, familiar lines about the need to take one little step, but the more he did so, the more I repeated the same phrase: 'You need a miracle. You need a miracle. You need a miracle.'

We must have spoken together for well over an hour, but gradually the truth dawned upon him. He came to the point where he realized that what was needed was not a small step by him, but a great miracle by God, and when he reached that place, and cried out to God to save him, God answered his prayer and the miracle took place.

Now what was true of that man (whose wife was converted soon afterwards) is true of every Christian. Each and every one begins his spiritual life with the

new birth — and the new birth is a miracle. It is tremendously important to grasp this. A man can tidy up
his old life, but he can never produce a new one. He
cannot buy it, earn it, or create it. As Jesus told Nicodemus, 'Flesh gives birth to flesh, but Spirit gives birth
to spirit' (John 3:6).

Does that grip your heart? Do you have any sense
of wonder that your spiritual life is the result of a
miracle? Are you so caught up with being a Christian
that you have forgotten how you became one? Are
you so busy trying to do things for the Lord that you
are no longer overawed by what he has done for you?
If so, an incident recorded in Luke's Gospel has an
important lesson for you. It concerns a staff conference
Jesus had with the seventy-two disciples he had sent
out on some form of evangelistic mission. We read,
'The seventy-two returned with joy, and said, "Lord,
even the demons submit to us in your name." He
replied, "I saw Satan fall like lightning from heaven.
I have given you authority to trample on snakes and
scorpions, and to overcome all the power of the enemy;
nothing will harm you. However, do not rejoice that
the spirits submit to you, but rejoice that your names
are written in heaven." ' Can you picture the scene?
These men had been given authority (the word *exousia*
we examined earlier) to cast out evil spirits and to work
miracles in the name of Jesus. Now, we can just imagine
them falling over each other to give their reports. They
were bursting to tell of the crowds, the meetings, the
response, the miracles and so on. But when they had
poured out all their news, Jesus told them there was
something that ought to cause them even greater joy,
and that was that '*your* names are written in heaven'.

Jesus knew the treachery of the human heart full
well. He knew that there was a very narrow dividing-
line between telling others what God had done through

them and telling them what they had done for God, so he lovingly turned their attention to the miracles of their own conversions.

There is a great lesson here. We should never allow ourselves to be so caught up with the work we are doing that we lose sight of the wonder of what we have become. *Ability in service is not as great a cause for rejoicing as authority in status.* The danger of dwelling too long on our Christian service is that we soon begin to speak as if we had done it by ourselves. The best antidote I know to that danger is to spend even longer meditating in amazement that our names are written in heaven, because we can be quite sure that we did nothing to contribute to that. As Paul says of our salvation, 'Where, then, is boasting? It is excluded' (Romans 3:27).

John Newton was a blasphemous and godless slave-trader, but he was dramatically converted, and later entered the Christian ministry. When he became the curate of Olney, in Buckinghamshire, he had parts of two verses of Scripture written above the mantelpiece in his study, the first from Isaiah 43:4 and the second from Deuteronomy 15:15. Put together (and updated to the NIV for uniformity) they read like this: 'Since you are precious and honoured in my sight . . . Remember that you were slaves in Egypt and the Lord your God redeemed you.' As Newton's reputation increased, so did the danger of forgetting the Lord's miraculous dealings in his life, but whenever he got away from the crowds and knelt alone in his study, he had before him those words, reminding him that although he had been gripped in the slavery of sin, he had been precious in God's sight and God in his utterly mysterious love had redeemed him and brought him to himself.

Find a place on the mantelpiece of your mind for that kind of truth! It will help to keep before you the

timeless truth that not only was your new birth into
the Christian family a mystery you cannot understand,
it was also a miracle you could not undertake.

3. The mark of being a son of God

We began this study by saying that spiritual life began
with new birth. We can now look at the same truth
from the opposite angle and say that the new birth is
always followed by new life. There is no such thing as
conversion without change: that is a contradiction in
terms. As Paul puts it so clearly, 'Therefore, if anyone
is in Christ, he is a new creation; the old has gone, the
new has come!' (2 Corinthians 5:17.) In other words,
the Christian is identified or marked out by a quality of
life utterly different from the one he lived before he was
converted.

I once took a week of meetings in a little log church
in Pinehurst, Idaho, way up in the north-west of the
United States. Every night, I noticed that in a congregation dressed largely in a very informal, country style,
there was an old man who always wore a very striking
bow tie. One night, he told me of his spiritual experience, and I discovered that the bow tie was not just to
prevent his shirt from falling open! He told me that as
a young man he became addicted to alcohol. Often,
when drunk, he became violently sick and his very wide
ties — they were in fashion at that time — were right
in the target area for 'matters arising'! Then he was
suddenly and dramatically converted. The grip that
alcohol had over him was instantly broken and, as he
put it to me, 'I promised the Lord that I would never
wear an ordinary tie again, and from then on my bow
tie is a reminder to me that I have put off the old life
and put on the new life. It is a mark of my conversion!'

That old man's unusual testimony took me straight to Paul's letter to the Colossians, where he writes, 'But now you must rid yourselves of all such things as these: anger, rage, malice, slander and filthy language from your lips. Do not lie to each other, since you have taken off your old self with its practices and have put on the new self, which is being renewed in knowledge in the image of its Creator' (Colossians 3:8–10). Paul's language here is the kind we would use about removing old or soiled clothing, and putting on clothes that are new or clean. The lesson is that God has given us a new wardrobe and he wants us to throw away the rotting rags we wore before we were converted. Now that we are Christians, what matters is not the character of our outward clothing, but the clothing of our inward character. A man may be poor or uneducated, he may be low down some people's assessment of the social scale, he may be unemployed or unemployable. He may be far from robust physically or have no obvious gifts of leadership. But the all-important thing is that if he is a Christian he should show that his 'new self' is 'being renewed in knowledge in the image of its Creator'.

To put that in another way, what Paul is saying is that God's children should bear the family likeness. Jesus emphasizes this in the sermon on the mount: 'You have heard that it was said, "Love your neighbour and hate your enemy." But I tell you, love your enemies and pray for those who persecute you, that you may be sons of your Father in heaven. He causes his sun to rise on the evil and the good, and sends rain on the righteous and the unrighteous.' Now, of course, Jesus is not saying that by behaving in a certain way a person *becomes* a child of God; that would mean that he was justified by works, not grace. What Jesus is saying is that loving behaviour by Christians means that they are *seen to be*

children of their heavenly Father, because he is a God
of love.

Notice how closely this ties in with the earlier part of
our study. It was when we were in open rebellion
against God that he lavished his saving love upon us.
When we were worth nothing, he gave us everything.
He loved us even when he could not look upon us.
That is how God acted towards us, and we are called
upon to demonstrate the fact that we are his children
by taking the same attitude towards all men, even our
enemies. Of course, we cannot save them as God saved
us, any more than we could save ourselves, but we are to
act in love towards them regardless of how they act
towards us. That is the point Jesus is making by giving
the illustration about God sending sun and rain on good
and evil men alike. God pours out these blessings on all
men without distinction, upon the downright sinner as
well as the upright saint. His gifts to men are not
governed by their gifts to him. What moves God to act
is what Dr Martyn Lloyd-Jones called 'his own eternal
heart of love unmoved by anything outside itself'.

What, then, is the overall distinguishing mark of the
Christian? We find the answer confirmed by reading on
a little further in Paul's letter to the Colossians: 'Therefore, as God's chosen people, holy and dearly loved,
clothe yourselves with compassion, kindness, humility,
gentleness and patience. Bear with each other and forgive whatever grievances you may have against one
another. Forgive as the Lord forgave you. And *over all
these virtues put on love,* which binds them all together
in perfect unity' (Colossians 3:12–14). What distin-
guishes one person from another when you see him in a
crowd is his outer garment, the article of clothing he
has put on over all the others. And Paul says that the
garment we ought to be wearing over all the others is
love. The mark of a son of God is that more and more

his actions towards his fellow men, even his enemies, are governed not by what these other people say, or do, or think, but by the unjudging love that is a reflection of the love of God in his own heart.

Do you have that mark? Do you have a loving concern for all men, even those who oppose you? Do you pray for those who persecute you? Do you seek to overcome evil with good? Do you constantly seek the highest good and the greatest blessing even of those people whose temperament prevents you from ever truly liking them? These are surely searching questions — but every professing Christian needs to face up to them, and to seek to respond to them in a way that will make a critical world take notice of his claim to be a child of God.

2.

A Saint
Separate and different

2.

A Saint
Separate and different

'ITALY TOPS THE SAINTS IN PARADISE LEAGUE.' That was the *Daily Telegraph* headline over an article that appeared in January 1974. A survey carried out by a Dutch Jesuit priest had apparently shown that of the 1,848 'registered' saints, 626 were Italians. France came second with 576, while the British Isles eased into bronze medal position with 271. Other revealing statistics of what was called 'official paradise' showed that over 1,000 of these saints were Catholic priests during their time on earth and that their number also included fifteen ex-popes, fourteen former married women and eight widowers.

All fascinating stuff, but unfortunately a very long way from biblical truth, because according to the Bible's clear teaching, to describe a person as a 'saint' is just another way of calling him a Christian. The point is made in many different ways, and nowhere more clearly than in the opening words of the apostle Paul's letter to the Ephesians, which he addresses to 'the saints in Ephesus, the faithful in Christ Jesus' (Ephesians 1:1). Although Paul uses two collective nouns here, he is obviously not referring to two different groups of people, one consisting of 'the saints in Ephesus' and the other 'the faithful in Christ Jesus'. Instead, he is describing one group of people in two different ways, and in so doing he tells us that the word 'saint' can

properly be applied to everyone who has come to a
living faith in the Lord Jesus Christ; in other words,
every Christian is a saint.

Yet the widespread misuse of the word over the
centuries has left Christians almost universally coy
about applying it to themselves. We are happy to call
ourselves 'believers', of course, or 'servants' or even
'children of God', but we are a little reluctant to call
ourselves 'saints'. When did you last hear someone
say, 'I am a saint'? Somehow, it sounds wrong, boastful,
arrogant. The subconscious feeling seeping through
centuries of misuse is that a saint is a particularly
good Christian, a kind of honours graduate in holy
living, a spiritual superstar. Yet all of this is thoroughly
unbiblical and has robbed us of a whole storehouse of
truth implicit in the fact that the Bible uses the word
'saint' of every Christian without exception. In this
study, then, let us try to recover the stolen property,
by examining three things that are implied by the fact
that the Bible describes all Christians as saints.

1. Our relationship to the Lord

The Greek word translated 'saint' in our Bibles is the
word *hagios*. The Hebrew equivalents are used over
800 times in the Old Testament, where they usually
have the primary meaning of 'separated', 'different',
'cut off' or 'set apart'. It is important to grasp this
clearly before we go any further, as the word's basic
root does not refer to moral goodness as opposed to
evil. It has not so much to do with the *quality* as with
the *nature* of a thing. We can confirm this by looking
briefly at some of the ways in which the basic word is
used.

For instance, *it is used of an article*. God's

instructions to Moses at Mount Sinai included the
following: 'Make *sacred* garments for your brother
Aaron, to give him dignity and honour' (Exodus 28:2).
Now the word translated 'sacred' is one of those Hebrew
equivalents of the New Testament word *hagios,* and the
point being made is not that Aaron's garments were to
be *cleaner* than any others (though we can be sure that
they would be spotlessly clean) but that they were to
be *different.* The material, design and ornamentation
were all to play their part in marking Aaron out as
holding a unique and God-appointed office.

Then, *it is used of a place.*   Part of the tabernacle
was called 'the Most *Holy* Place' (Leviticus 16:2).
Here, the phrase 'Most Holy' translates the word we
are studying, and again the point about its use is surely
obvious. This very special part of the tabernacle was
not described in this way because it was the best kept,
or most hygienic (however true that might have been)
but because it was curtained off from the remainder of
the building. It was separate, cut off, different, apart
from the rest.

Thirdly, *it is used of a period of time.*   In the story
of the creation, we read, 'And God blessed the seventh
day and made it *holy,* because on it he rested from all
the work of creating that he had done' (Genesis 2:3).
This time, the key word is translated 'holy' (as *hagios*
often is in the New Testament also), and the obvious
suggestion is not that the seventh day was in any way
better than the other six, but rather that it was different. God performed all his mighty acts of creation
on the first six days, but on the seventh he acted differently.

Now there is an obvious link between those three
uses of the same basic word. Aaron's garments were
made differently at God's command; the Most Holy
Place was cut off from the remainder of the tabernacle

according to God's blueprint; the sabbath, or seventh day, became different by God's decree. They were all different *because God himself is different.* He is utterly separate and apart from the whole of his universe. This comes across in one of the questions God asks in the Old Testament: ' "To whom will you compare me? Or who is my equal?" says the *Holy* One' (Isaiah 40:25). The question is unanswerable because God is incomparable. His very names and nature tell us that he is different, separate, distinct, unique — and one of the Bible's great words for that particular property is the word 'holy'.

When Isaiah had his amazing vision of the Lord, he spoke of celestial beings crying one to another and saying, 'Holy, holy, holy is the Lord Almighty; the whole earth is full of his glory' (Isaiah 6:3). In only one other place in Scripture do we find a description of God raised, as it were, to the power of three, and that is where once more celestial beings cry out in adoration, 'Holy, holy, holy is the Lord God Almighty who was, and is, and is to come' (Revelation 4:8). In both cases, what is being said is not merely that God is righteous, pure and perfect (though the word 'holy' has gathered about it all of those connotations) but that he is utterly and essentially removed from every other being in the entire universe.

Pursuing the use of the word a little further, it is interesting to notice that it is used about all three Persons in the Godhead. In the course of his remarkable prayer recorded in John 17, Jesus said, 'I will remain in the world no longer, but they are still in the world, and I am coming to you. *Holy Father,* protect them by the power of your name — the name you gave me — so that they may be one as we are one' (John 17:11). Some time later, when the disciples met for praise and prayer after the release of Peter and John from prison, they prayed that they might be given great boldness to preach in the face of their enemies, then went on, 'Stretch out your hand to heal and perform miraculous signs and wonders through the name of *your holy servant Jesus*' (Acts 4:30). Finally, of course, the third Person in the Godhead is almost invariably called 'the Holy Spirit'.

Here, then, is the great, characteristic word used about God. He is 'holy' — different, separate from all else and all others, and this is where we must begin if we are to have a biblical understanding of what it is to be 'holy', to be a 'saint'. The word principally points to *a special relationship with God*. To go back to our three original illustrations, Aaron's garments were to be used exclusively for God's worship; the Most Holy Place was set aside for that same sacred purpose; the seventh day was to be a unique opportunity for acknowledging the Lord's glory and showing forth his praise. All three were called 'holy' because of their relationship to God.

The same is true when the word is used about people. It speaks firstly of relationship. When a person becomes a Christian he becomes a saint, because he enters into a new, vital and personal relationship with God. In my native island of Guernsey there is a beautiful spot on the coast called Saints Bay, a name we locals often abbreviate to 'Saints'. I remember an occasion when I caught a bus from St Peter Port to go there. As the bus drew away, two or three people came running towards the terminus. Unsure as to whether or not they wanted to board his particular bus, our driver leaned out of the window and shouted 'Saints?' When they shook their heads and made for another bus, the driver turned to us and said laughingly, 'Then they must be sinners!' The story is not told to prove that all Guernsey bus drivers are theologians — but at least that one did make a precise biblical point at that moment! Every person in the world is either a saint or a sinner, and the saints are those who have come into a living relationship with God through faith in the Lord Jesus Christ.

It is interesting to contrast this biblical picture of a person becoming a saint with the one traditionally taught by the Roman Catholic Church. Firstly, that church canonizes a person only after his death; the Bible teaches that a person becomes a saint while still alive. Traditional Catholic teaching is that a saint is elected by the church, a biblical saint is one chosen by the Lord. An ecclesiastical saint is made as a result of good works; the Bible teaches that a person is made a saint in spite of bad works. In creating a saint, the Catholic church looks for miracles performed by the person concerned; in the Bible, we are taught that a person becomes a saint because of a miracle worked by God *in* the person concerned. What contrasts! In the one case, the all-important thing is recognition by the church; in the other, the all-important thing is relationship to the Lord. Such is the complicated mess man gets into when he strays from the simplicity and beauty of the gospel.

Our point is made even clearer when we realize that almost every time it is used in the Old Testament there is a statement or inference about the believer's relationship to the Lord. What is more, that relationship is shown to be not only personal, vital and special, but *eternal*. This comes across in David's words: 'Precious in the sight of the Lord is the death of his saints' (Psalm 116:15). To the unbeliever, 'precious' must seem a strange word to use in connection with death. After all, death is a very solemn thing, often accompanied by great pain, agony and sorrow on the part both of the dying and the bereaved. But the Bible teaches that

we need never grieve over the death of a Christian
'like the rest of men, who have no hope' (1 Thessalonians 4:13) because of our assurance that at death
the Christian passes into the immediate presence of
the Lord. The believer's death may, of course, be painful for those of us who mourn on a human level, but as
far as God is concerned it is actually 'precious', because
one of his saints, one of his children, a member of his
family, one of those for whom Christ died, has come
home, to remain in his glorious presence for ever. The
saint's relationship with the Lord is one that lasts
throughout life, through death and into eternity. To be
a saint is to be in an eternal relationship with the Lord.

2. Our discipleship in the world

It would be fascinating to go through the Bible with a
fine tooth-comb to discover how many things we are
told about the character, nature and attributes of God.
Yet they could all be summarized in one statement of
just three words. It would be equally interesting to
discover how many commandments, negative and
positive, the Bible gives to Christians to guide them in
the conduct of their daily lives. They must run into
multiplied hundreds — yet they could be summarized
in one statement of just two words. Even more
amazingly, both groups of words come together in a
single sentence, where the apostle Peter gathers together
several Old Testament statements into one all-embracing
demand which God makes upon his people: 'Be holy,
because I am holy' (1 Peter 1:16). It would surely be
impossible to put a description of God and a summary
of his demands upon men into fewer words than that.
We might almost call it a transistorized version of God's
moral law. The simplest way to describe God is to say

that he is holy; the simplest way to describe his require-
ments for us is to say that he commands us to be holy.
Commenting on this verse, Alan Stibbs wrote, 'So the
first and sufficient reason why God's people should
keep themselves from uncleanness is because the Lord
their God is holy; only so can they respond to their
calling and enjoy intimate fellowship with him. It is,
therefore, the revelation of God's character and the call
to be intimately related to him that makes holiness an
obligation.' I like that! Our discipleship is demanded by
the very nature of the One with whom we are in such a
wonderful relationship. When a Christian asks, 'Why
should I behave differently from my unconverted
friends?' the answer is 'Because you *are* different'!
In other words, Scripture demands that the Christian's
practice should correspond to his position: a saint
should be saintly. In Matthew Henry's words, ' "Be
ye holy" is the great and fundamental law of our
religion.' Let us pursue that a little further, both negatively and positively.

Firstly, the negative aspect.   Writing to the Ephesians,
Paul says, 'Be imitators of God, therefore, as dearly
loved children and live a life of love, just as Christ loved
us and gave himself up for us as a fragrant offering and
sacrifice to God. But among you there must not be even
a hint of sexual immorality, or of any kind of impurity,
or of greed, because these are improper for God's holy
people' (Ephesians 5:1–3). Paul's point is clear. There
are certain actions that are plainly not right for Christians. These things may represent the normal social
standards of a basically godless society, but a saint is
different, and is to behave differently.

I will never forget the first time I came across one
particular verse in the New Testament. I was a young
Christian at the time, and whole areas of the Bible were
completely new to me. Then one day I read these words

(in the old Authorized Version, which I was then using): 'We know that whosoever is born of God sinneth not' (1 John 5:18). I was flabbergasted! What on earth was the Bible saying? I was sure that I was a Christian, but I was equally sure that no one could say of me, 'He sinneth not'! Only by delving a little did I discover the tense of John's verb and the sense of his statement. All of this is helpfully clarified in the New International Version, which reads, 'We know that anyone born of God does not *continue* to sin.' John does not mean that a Christian does not commit even one isolated act of sin. That would make nonsense of Christ's command to the disciples to pray, 'Forgive us our sins' (Luke 11:4), and would even contradict what John himself wrote earlier in this same letter: 'If we claim to be without sin, we deceive ourselves and the truth is not in us' (1 John 1:8).

What John is really saying is that the general tenor, thrust and direction of a Christian's life are away from sin. He does not gladly and habitually continue in sinful ways. I remember once discussing this verse with Mrs Mary Wood, a distinguished member of that remarkable family of Woods whose influence through the National Young Life Campaign has enriched my life and the lives of countless other people. After we had discussed the theological background, and had a stab at the Greek tenses and other technicalities, she suddenly turned to me and said, 'John, what this verse really means is that, for the Christian, *sin is not the done thing.*' I must say that I find it very difficult to improve on that! It is not the done thing. It is out of character. An Old Testament illustration will help to drive this home. When Nehemiah, dedicated to carry through the task God had given him to do, was advised to escape when his life was in danger, his reply was instant and characteristic: 'Should a man like me run away?' (Nehemiah 6:11.)

God had called him to be a man of courage; how could he turn coward? Nehemiah recognized that his behaviour must be related to his divinely appointed position, and every Christian should have a similar sense of discipleship. Negatively, then, to be a saint entails the discipline of resisting temptation and rejecting sin at every turn, because to do otherwise is to act out of character with our very name.

Secondly, the positive aspect. This is succinctly stated by Paul in these words: 'For God did not call us to be impure but to live a holy life' (1 Thessalonians 4:7). A holy God calls people to holy living; it is inconceivable that it should be otherwise. As Professor R. A. Finlayson says, 'The New Testament everywhere emphasizes the ethical nature of holiness in contrast to all uncleanness. It is represented as the supreme vocation of Christians and the goal of their living.' Here is the positive aspect of saintly living and it is important to stress that the Christian life *is* positive. The Christian's code of conduct does include important negatives, of course — eight of the Ten Commandments make this clear — but the biblical concept of a Christian life is essentially a matter of positive goodness.

The story is told of a pastor who tended to major on the negative, 'thou-shalt-not' aspect of the Christian life. On one occasion he took the morning service in a little country church, and later went to lunch with a member of the congregation who was a farmer. After lunch, the farmer told the minister, 'I would like you to come and meet my donkey.' Not wishing to offend his host, the preacher agreed, but asked why the farmer was apparently so keen on the idea. 'Because my donkey is a Christian,' the farmer replied. 'Don't be ridiculous,' the pastor retorted, 'no donkey can be a Christian.' 'Well, according to your sermon this morning, it can,' the farmer said. 'My donkey doesn't swear, drink alcohol, smoke tobacco or work on Sundays, so I reckon that according to your sermon it must be a Christian!'

Hopefully, the story is apocryphal, but it is not without point. God's call is not merely to empty our lives of sin, but to fill them with righteousness. As the writer to the Hebrews says, we are to *'make every effort* to live in peace with all men and *to be holy'* (Hebrews 12:14), while Peter adds that if a man would know God's blessing on his life he must 'turn from evil *and do good'* (1 Peter 3:11). Positive Christian discipleship is the vocation to which we are called. John Newton, the converted slave-trader, once put it like this, in words which it would be difficult to better outside of Scripture: 'Christ has taken our nature into heaven, to represent us, and has left us on earth, with his nature, to represent him.' To be a saint, then, not only means relationship with the Lord, it also demands discipleship in the world.

3. Our fellowship in the church

It is surely a remarkable fact that although the word *hagios* as a definition of a Christian is used over sixty times in the New Testament it is never used in the singular. The lesson seems crystal clear. No Christian is meant to go it alone, to live in isolation from other Christians. While it is true that every Christian comes to Christ as an individual, it is equally true that from the moment of his conversion he is in fellowship with every other Christian in the world. The Christian faith is intensely personal, but is never private. As Paul wrote to the Christians at Ephesus, 'You are no longer foreigners and aliens, but fellow-citizens with God's people and members of God's household' (Ephesians 2:19).

This heavenly household includes in its earthly

members all Christians of all ages, all levels of wealth
and intelligence, all nationalities and all levels of social
strata. As Paul tells the Galatians, 'There is neither Jew
nor Greek, slave nor free, male nor female, for you are
all one in Christ Jesus' (Galatians 3:28). A friend of
mine was once taking a series of meetings in a town I
know well — Katerini, in northern Greece. One evening
he was on the verandah of the church's orphanage,
photographing the sunset, when a Greek workman,
whom he rightly took to be a Christian, happened to
join him. The language barrier was impassable, but my
friend was determined to do something to express the
sense of Christ-centered fellowship that he felt in his
heart. Pointing to the flaming glory of the sunset over
the mountains, he looked at the workman and said,
'Jesus!' Next, he pointed to the spire of the church a
few yards away and said, 'Jesus!' Then his arm pointed
straight into the sky as he repeated the one word,
'Jesus!' Finally, he put one hand over the workman's
heart and the other over his own while the wondrous
word said it all — 'Jesus!' Their backgrounds, cultures
and languages could hardly have been more different,
but in that delightful moment they each knew that they
were fellow-citizens with all God's people everywhere.

Yet that striking example was something special. In
those somewhat emotional circumstances, we might
easily do the same kind of thing. The real test comes
when we are on familiar home ground, among Christians whose language, background, circumstances, fail-
ings (and business in general!) we know only too well.
The cynic was sadly too near the truth when he wrote,

> To dwell above with saints we love,
> Oh my, that will be glory!
> To dwell below, with saints we know,
> Well, that's another story!

As we have seen, the Bible tells us that we are *'all* one

in Christ Jesus'. That sounds fine in theory, but remember that it brings you into relationship with *all* your fellow-Christians, including those who hold to different interpretations of certain passages of Scripture, those whose life-style cuts across yours, and even those who do not have the native intelligence to agree with you on matters of church policy! It is here, at the local, grass-root level, that we are most often called upon to demonstrate the reality of our oneness in Christ. Nor is it enough to go around repeating Galatians 3:28 to each other. The real challenge is to demonstrate the reality of our fellowship by such things as sympathy, understanding, prayer, ready forgiveness, reluctance to criticize, practical help when it is needed and not only when it is asked for, and a willingness to act as a family in dealing with individual and corporate needs in the church. As William Hendriksen puts it, 'Everybody should put his shoulder under the burdens under which this or that individual member is groaning, whatever these burdens may be. They must be carried jointly.'

What a vast area of thought that opens up! The need may be for financial assistance, for help in looking after children in an emergency, for home care at a time of sickness or disability, for sympathy and understanding in an hour of grief, for unjudging help in recovering from a moral fall. The list is endless, and the call is obvious. The fact of our fellowship makes inevitable, practical and inescapable demands upon us. We are saints *together*.

I sometimes receive letters from Christians who sign off with the phrase, 'Yours because his'; and the expression is simply yet profoundly true. As Christians, we belong to each other because we first belong to the Lord. In other words, our fellowship in the church is directly linked to our relationship with the Lord. This link is beautifully expressed by Paul when he tells the

Romans that 'In Christ, we who are many form one body, and each member belongs to all the others' (Romans 12:5). That one statement speaks not only of our great privilege as Christians in forming individual parts of the body of Christ, the Christian church, it speaks also of our deep, searching responsibility to every other Christian in the world, regardless of race, colour, age or denomination. We are bound to one another in a fellowship that goes far beyond the mere sharing of a common interest, hobby or political affiliation. What binds us together is a supernatural reality that carries with it the responsibility of Christ-like, caring love.

Only when we learn to enjoy that kind of fellowship, show that kind of love, and bear one another's burdens in such a sympathetic way will we be fulfilling as we should our vocation as saints.

3.

A Sheep
The Shepherd's care

3.

A Sheep
The Shepherd's care

When does a sheep give an impersonation of a horse or a
donkey? To unravel this unlikely conundrum we need to
go to the heart of the Old Testament, where God gives
this unusual and striking command: 'Do not be like the
horse or the mule, which have no understanding, but
must be controlled by bit and bridle . . .' (Psalm 32:9).
What vivid pictures these are! A horse is an impetuous,
headstrong animal, always wanting to plunge forward in
its own way, whereas a mule, or donkey, always seems
to want to dig in its heels, obstinately refusing to budge;
and that particular part of the psalm, which is about
being guided by God in one's daily life, is warning the
Christian about the dangers of dashing ahead in his own
impetuous enthusiasm or of lagging behind God's
purposes for his life in hesitant unbelief.

In other words, the Christian must not act like a horse
or a donkey — and what makes either kind of behaviour
even more inappropriate is that in biblical terminology
the Christian is described not as a horse or a donkey, but
as a sheep! It is this particular picture of a Christian that
we are going to study in this chapter, and we will do so
by giving our main attention to one part of Scripture.
The picture of a Christian as a sheep is used in the
Psalms, in Isaiah, in Ezekiel and in several places in the
New Testament, but we shall concentrate on part of one
chapter in John's Gospel, with occasional reference to
what is probably the best-known passage in the Old
Testament, Psalm 23.

   The first thing to notice is that both of these passages
have the same focal point or centre of gravity. The more
you read them, the more obvious it becomes that they
are not essentially about the sheep, but about the
Shepherd! In Psalm 23, everything else flows from the
opening statement, 'The Lord is my shepherd', and in
John 10 the same truth is crystallized in Jesus' words:
'I am the good shepherd.' In other words, the emphasis
in both places is not so much on what the sheep ought
to do, but on what the Shepherd has done and is doing
for the sheep. It is striking that there is not a single
imperative in either passage, not one thing that we are
told to do or not to do. Instead, both passages are
encouraging expositions of the divine Shepherd's activities on behalf of his sheep, and not least his careful
and loving provision for them. In this chapter, then,
let us look at some of these activities and at what the
implications are for us in our daily lives.

1. Salvation

To begin here is to begin at the beginning! In biblical
terms, the first thing the shepherd provides for the
sheep is salvation, with all that that marvellous word
implies. In the early part of Christ's earthly ministry,
we read that 'When he saw the crowds, he had compassion on them, because they were harassed and helpless,
like sheep without a shepherd' (Matthew 9:36) and
there are two ways of getting at the truth of what this
means. The first is to take a closer look at the word
used to describe the crowds. The word translated
'harassed' includes the sense of being bewildered and
confused, of not knowing which way to turn. The word
translated 'helpless' literally means 'thrown down', and
pictures people depressed, dejected and demoralized.

The second way of understanding what is being said here is by pursuing the very illustration the words give. In the Middle East, a shepherd is usually the owner of a very small flock of sheep, which he *leads* from one place to another. In more fertile lands, the shepherd *follows* the sheep. providing fresh pasture for them is usually just a question of transferring them from one grassy field to another; all the shepherd has to do is to open a gate and encourage the sheep to drift in the right direction. But in the Middle East the picture is different. Green pasture is scattered and scarce, and the sheep have no instinct as to where it might be found. What happens, therefore, is that the shepherd, with his knowledge of the area, goes in front, finds the pastures and watering places, and then leads the sheep to them.

Now the illustration is becoming clear. To put it bluntly, without a shepherd, the sheep would be mutton! No shepherd — no grass; no grass — no food; no food — no life. It is therefore literally true that for the sheep, the shepherd means life. And Jesus saw the people around him 'like sheep without a shepherd'. In other words, they were spiritually dead, and without him they were without any hope of spiritual life. Here is a bedrock, fundamental truth. The first thing the shepherd gives the sheep is life. When Jesus said, 'I have come that they may have life' (John 10:10), he did not mean that he had come merely to give men a new dimension to life, or to guide men's lives into more lively avenues of usefulness — *but to give them life.*

The Bible could not be clearer at this point. Left to himself, man is spiritually dead, 'without hope and without God in the world' (Ephesians 2:12). In Isaiah's words, 'We all, like sheep, have gone astray, each of us has turned to his own way' (Isaiah 53:6). What this says is that the unconverted is deliberately off course, he is wilfully wayward. He has chosen to die in a wilderness of his own making, and unless the Good Shepherd comes to his rescue he is doomed for ever. Only when we grasp this can we grasp the significance of the birth, life, death and resurrection of the Lord Jesus Christ. These events were not the component parts of an elaborate publicity campaign for higher moral standards; *Christ was on a rescue mission.*

Going back to John 10, we find the additional and amazing truth that Christ secured the Christian's life at the cost of his own. As he himself put it, 'The good shepherd lays down his life for the sheep' (John 10:11) and again, 'I lay down my life for the sheep' (John 10:15). Jesus did not come into this world on some vague goodwill enterprise, he came for the specific and predetermined purpose of dying in the place of 'the sheep', his own chosen people, in order that their sins might be put away and that they might receive the gift of eternal life. The angel's prophecy to Joseph before the birth of Jesus was clear and definite: 'You are to give him the name Jesus, because he will save his people from their sins' (Matthew 1:21). This was no tentative possibility. The death of Jesus was not a proposition to sinners; it was a plan of salvation, and because it was God's plan *it worked!* With unerring certainty, the Holy Spirit draws to saving faith in Christ all those for whom the Saviour died, so that every Christian in the world can echo the words of Philip Bliss's great hymn:

Bearing shame and scoffing rude,
In my place condemned he stood;
Sealed my pardon with his blood;
Hallelujah! What a Saviour!

Are you rejoicing in that certainty? Are you sure that Christ died in *your* place, bearing *your* sin? Can you say with David, 'The Lord is *my* shepherd'? That is where the Christian life begins!

2. Sensitivity

Not only does the Lord give his spiritual sheep salvation, he also gives them sensitivity in a number of different areas. There are several references to this in John 10. In the first, Jesus uses the natural illustration, and says that when the shepherd comes to the communal sheepfold and opens the gate 'the sheep listen to his voice' (John 10:3). He then goes on to say that when the shepherd has collected all his own sheep 'he goes on ahead of them, and his sheep follow him because they know his voice. But they will never follow a stranger; in fact, they will run away from him because they do not recognize a stranger's voice' (John 10:4—5). Later on, he applies this truth spiritually and says, 'My sheep listen to my voice, I know them and they follow me' (John 10:27). But in spiritual terms this sensitivity is not something natural to the sheep; it is something given by the shepherd, and it is when we begin to follow this through that we begin to understand something of its importance.

Firstly, it is important in our hearing of the gospel. Did you come to put your faith in Christ the very first time you heard the gospel? Almost certainly not. You probably heard the gospel many times before you actually responded to it in repentance and faith. Then came that all-important day (even if you cannot pinpoint it now) when you heard the message not only with your outward ears, but with what we might call your spiritual ears, when you accepted the message you had hitherto rejected. Then what was it that made the difference? Just this, that the Lord tuned you in to the truth, he made you receptive to the message. Let me focus this picture a little more closely, somewhat along the lines

we noticed when studying the truth that a Christian is
a son of God. If you were converted in a meeting or
service of some kind, there were almost certainly unconverted people there who heard exactly the same
preacher, sang the same hymns, joined in the 'Amens' at
the end of the same prayers. Can you explain why these
other people were unmoved by what was said, while
you responded in such a way? Can you explain why
you said, 'Yes', to Christ while they said, 'No'? The
difference was this: they heard the preacher's voice,
but you heard the Lord's voice. And the reason you
were able to hear that voice and recognize and respond
to it was that the Lord himself made you sensitive to it.

The New Testament story of Lydia's conversion is
a clear illustration of this. Paul and Silas were in Philippi
as part of one of their missionary journeys, and attended
some kind of open-air prayer meeting by the side of
a river. As they shared the gospel message with the
people, one of those who heard them was a local trades-
woman by the name of Lydia. The Bible says that as
Paul was preaching, 'The Lord opened her heart to
respond to Paul's message' (Acts 16:14). In other words,
the Lord gave her *sensitivity*. He graciously enabled
her to grasp the significance of what was being said, and
to respond to it in repentance and faith. It is unfortunately true to say that a great deal of so-called evangelistic preaching today gives the impression that the
unconverted sinner has the power to open his own
heart, with an impotent Christ waiting forlornly outside
the door in frustrated suspense, waiting for the sinner
to do him a favour. But nothing could be further from
the truth, and every Christian should rejoice in the fact
that the only way in which he was able to be saved was
that, in his great mercy, the Lord gave him sensitivity
to hear and understand the gospel.

Secondly, it is important in our understanding of the

Bible. I am not suggesting, of course, that any Christian understands the meaning of every passage, phrase and word of the Bible (not even those who give the impression that they do!) but the fact remains that God does give his people a spiritual understanding of his Word, one which they could not possibly have if left to their own resources. One of the loveliest incidents recorded in the New Testament illustrates this beautifully. On the first Easter Day, two disciples of Jesus were walking to Emmaus. Suddenly, they were joined by Jesus, though they did not recognize him. As they continued their walk, the three spoke together about the tremendous events of the previous days, the disciples even telling Jesus about reports of the tomb being empty with (as it seemed to them) no confirmatory evidence of a rumour that Jesus had returned to life.

At that point, Jesus began to explain to them why these momentous events were a necessary fulfilment of prophecy: 'And beginning with Moses and all the Prophets, he explained to them what was said in all the Scriptures concerning himself' (Luke 24:27). The effect was electrifying, and when he finally left them, they turned to each other and said, 'Were not our hearts burning within us while he talked with us on the road and opened the Scriptures to us?' (Luke 24:32.) Notice the significance of this. Until the Lord opened their spiritual eyes to the meaning of Scripture, not even his death and resurrection had any true meaning to them! Overwhelmed by what they now knew, they rushed to Jerusalem to share the news with the other disciples. But while they were telling their story, Jesus appeared again. After assuring them all that he really had risen from the dead, he explained once more that his death and resurrection were an essential fulfilment of Old Testament prophecy, and 'he opened their minds so they could understand the Scriptures' (Luke 24:45). He gave them sensitivity to the truth of the Bible's teaching.

It is tremendously important that you grasp what this means to you as a Christian. When Jesus was warning his disciples of his approaching death, he promised that when he had gone into heaven they would receive the Holy Spirit, and added that 'When he, the Spirit of truth, comes, he will guide you into all truth' (John 16:13). Through the Holy Spirit, God has promised to give Christians an understanding of his Word, a sensitivity to the truth. What a great encouragement this is! You may not be an expert, a scholar, a linguist, or a theologian, but if you are a Christian, then God has promised you that the Holy Spirit is available to you and can enable you to understand what the Bible means and to apply its truth to your heart and life. I know of nothing more exciting than to come away from a time of Bible study knowing that God has spoken to *me* through its pages, that words written thousands of years ago have come alive for *me*, in my own life and circumstances. It is thrilling, electrifying! J.B. Phillips used exactly this kind of picture in the Preface to his book *Letters to Young Churches,* a paraphrase of the New Testament Epistles. He wrote that while he was at work on the book, 'Again and again the writer felt rather like an electrician re-wiring an ancient house without being able to "turn the mains off".'

Christians should always be praying for that kind of sensitivity as they read the Bible. It is marvellous beyond words than in spite of our ignorance, our immaturity and all our other failures we can turn to the Bible and hear the Lord's voice as clearly as if the Lord Jesus were standing physically alongside us. Such an experience is not the result of reasoning, nor of research, but of revelation — God making himself known to us, giving us a sensitivity to his Word.

Thirdly, it is important in the matter of conscience.
Somebody once described conscience as 'a still, small
voice that makes minority reports', but the truth lies
deeper than that. John Calvin was much more to the
point when he said, 'Distinction between virtuous
and vicious actions has been engraven by the Lord on
the heart of every man.' So was Matthew Henry when
he wrote, 'Conscience is that candle of the Lord which
was not quite put out.' This is much more in line with
the general drift of the Bible's teaching, which is that
when a person becomes a Christian, God sensitizes
his conscience, so that the more the Christian grows in
his knowledge of the Bible and in the grace of God, the
more clearly he recognizes the difference between right
and wrong. To go back to the illustration from nature in
John 10, the more mature a sheep becomes, the more
clearly it learns to recognize the voice of the shepherd
and to turn away from the dangerous voice of the
stranger.

I love the story of the fairly new Christian who
attended a conference held at Hildenborough Hall, in
Kent, and conducted by that very fine evangelist and
Bible teacher Tom Rees. On the last day there was a
testimony session, at which guests were invited to share
something of what they had learned during the conference. This man apparently brought the house down
by saying, 'Mr Rees, I just want you to know that I
never realized what sin really was until I came to Hildenborough Hall'! No doubt Tom Rees, with his ready
sense of humour, made a meal of that — but of course
the man was actually making a serious and very important point. Under the teaching of God's Word he had
become much more sensitive in his conscience, and as
a result he had a much clearer picture of sin's serious-
ness, subtlety and power.

The lessons to be drawn from all of this are simple

yet important. Every Christian should seek to develop that kind of sensitivity and pray for an increasing ability to recognize the voice of the Lord and to ignore the voice of any 'stranger' who would lead him into disobedience, danger or disgrace. The Lord's gracious gift of sensitivity is an important factor in making spiritual progress.

3. Sustenance

This third provision by the shepherd for the sheep is very closely connected with the area we have just been studying, and we establish its basis by going back once again to John 10. There we find Jesus saying this: 'I am the gate, whoever enters through me will be saved. He will come in and go out and find pasture' (John 10:9). This blends in exactly with a statement in the other 'shepherd' passage we are bearing in mind. Psalm 23, where David's testimony is 'He makes me lie down in green pastures, he leads me beside quiet waters' (Psalm 23:2).

In physical life there are three basic essentials to good health — food (and drink), exercise and rest — which together provide what we could in general terms call sustenance for the body. In the two passages of Scripture before us we have spiritual parallels. For food and drink we have 'green pastures' and 'still waters', for exercise we 'come in and go out' and for rest we 'lie down'. Now while we may not press an exegesis of those phrases quite as closely as that, what *is* plain from these two passages, and indeed from Scripture as a whole, is that the Lord, having saved his sheep and given them sensitivity to his voice, also provides all that they need for their daily and lifelong spiritual sustenance.

No Christian ought to doubt that! Jesus is no mere

part-time shepherd, hired to do an irksome job but with
no heart for it and no personal interest in it. He is the
Good Shepherd, who so loves the sheep that he gives
his life for them. Is it even remotely likely that such a
shepherd would ever leave his beloved sheep without
sustenance? Paul asks this kind of question when writing
to the Romans: 'If God is for us, who can be against us?
He who did not spare his own Son, but gave him up for
us all — how will he not also, along with him, graciously give us all things?' (Romans 8:31—32.) That
passage comes in a part of Romans written in the specific context of Christians suffering in the world, Paul
reminding his readers that as far as the world is concerned, 'we are considered as sheep to be slaughtered'
(Romans 8:36). It is as he visualizes the Christian
defenceless and helpless against the pressures of an evil
world, the treachery of his own heart and the remorse-
less attacks of the devil that Paul assures him of God's
gracious provision of 'all things'.

We may feel as helpless as sheep in a world overrun
by ravenous wolves, but as surely as the Good Shepherd
has died to give us eternal life, just as surely is he with
us day by day to provide our every need, to lavish upon
us all he has to give.

4. Satisfaction

This takes our last point a little further. We could say
that satisfaction speaks of a conscious enjoyment of
God's goodness, and again we will find the basis for this
in our two chosen passages of Scripture. Firstly, we find
Jesus saying, 'I have come that they may have life and
have it to the full' (John 10:10), while David testifies,
'The Lord is my shepherd, I shall lack nothing' adding
a little later, 'My cup overflows' (Psalm 23:1, 5).

Somebody once said, 'There are two things I have always looked upon as difficult. The one is to make the wicked sad and the other is to make the godly joyful!' As a preacher, I can certainly identify with the first of those problems, and know more than a little of the problem of bringing conviction of sin to those who reject God, but it is surely a tragedy when Christians find it difficult to be joyful.

There is something wrong with Christians who give the impression that holiness is to be measured by the length of their faces. Of course, there are those who appear to go to the other extreme, who seem to measure sanctification by smiles and godliness by grins, and who appear to be saying that unless you are leaping about in the aisles, or at the very least singing a happy chorus all day long and generally bubbling over with the prescribed amount of evangelical effervescence you are spiritually sub-normal. That is nonsense, of course, but I am equally sure that every Christian should seek for a deep, conscious and continuous enjoyment of the Lord's gracious presence. The first question asked in the Westminster Assembly's Shorter Catechism (1647) is this: 'What is the chief end of man?' to which the answer is 'Man's chief end is to glorify God and to *enjoy* him for ever.' Every Christian should seek to live in the spirit of that reply!

No Christian ought to find life in today's world easy or undemanding, because he is living in an alien environment, surrounded by problems, tensions, trials, stresses, difficulties and temptations on every hand. But neither should he go around giving the impression that the Christian life is dull, burdensome, restrictive and unsatisfying. I can think of some Christians whose general demeanour is so lugubrious that if I were unconverted I would not go within a mile of them in case I caught what they had! But we are meant to *enjoy* our salvation, not endure it! And the secret of living a responsible, caring life in today's world, and yet doing so with an inner radiance that commends our faith to others, is to allow nothing to come between us and a daily pre-occupation with *the Lord himself.* As the psalmist says, '*He* satisfies the thirsty and fills the hungry with good things' (Psalm 107:9).

But this needs following through a little. There are many earthly pleasures that we can genuinely enjoy — physical, mental, cultural, artistic, social and so on — and these may be perfectly legitimate, honest and commendable. It is the devil's lie that the worlds of music, art and sport, to name but three, are entirely and intrinsically 'worldly', part of a humanistic culture, not things that can be wholly committed to the Lord or enjoyed with his unreserved blessing. That is nonsense. The Bible teaches that God 'richly provides us with everything for our enjoyment' (1 Timothy 6:17) and to limit 'everything' to the realm of the theological or even the spiritual is to become the impoverished victim of mis-guided zeal. The simple and liberating truth is that 'every good and perfect gift is from above, coming down from the Father of the heavenly lights' (James 1:17) and those gifts include those given to unconverted men who, for all their unbelief, are nevertheless 'made in God's like-ness' (James 3:9). To attempt to shut ourselves off from these gifts and these people is to refuse God's open-handed goodness because of our short-sighted prejudice.

Yet having said that, it remains true that no enjoy-ment of culture, the arts, sport and the like can ever bring us complete *satisfaction,* for the simple reason that man is more than cultural, artistic and sporting. These activities may relax us, exhilarate us, or refresh us, but they can never truly *satisfy* us, even when they promise to do so. Some years ago I was playing at the Black Mountain Golf Club, North Carolina (the golfing

'home' of Billy Graham), when I came across this
couplet in the professional's shop:

My only wish afore I go to heaven,
It to come in just once with a sixty-seven.

As a golfing enthusiast, every sporting cell in my body
yearns to do just that! But I know perfectly well that
even if I did, it would not satisfy me. There is more to
life than breaking par, or even breaking records, and
there is infinitely more to man's make-up than that
which can find ultimate satisfaction in culture, sport
or the arts. Man is essentially *spiritual* and it is only
at that level that he can ever find true satisfaction. But
we must go further than that and say that he will not
find such satisfaction in religious or Christian 'things',
nor even in Christian activity or service. The Christian's
true spiritual satisfaction is only to be found in *the Lord
himself,* and the promise of God's Word is that 'Those
who seek *the Lord* lack no good thing' (Psalm 34:10).
Let that truth settle down deep into your heart and
seek to have your life so preoccupied with *him* that you
will know what it is to be 'filled to the measure of all
the fulness of God' (Ephesians 3:19).

5. Security

This final word in our study of the Good Shepherd's
provision for his sheep is one of the great themes woven
into both John 10 and Psalm 23 and which speak of
security in two ways.

Firstly, there is earthly security. In John 10, Jesus
speaks of the dangers to the flock when attacked by
a wolf. He says that a hired hand would run away,
leaving the flock to be ravaged, but then assures his
people, 'I am the good shepherd' (John 10:11, 14),
inferring that he will never leave his flock alone,

unprotected or insecure. In Psalm 23 David says, 'You
prepare a table before me in the presence of my enemies'
(Psalm 23:5) and a moment later adds, 'Surely goodness
and love will follow me all the days of my life' (Psalm
23:6). We could call this 'earthly security', the promise
of God's presence and protection no matter how great
or powerful our earthly enemies may be. When Adon-
iram Judson went out as a missionary to Burma early
in the nineteenth century he was captured by ruthless
natives, strung up by his thumbs, tortured and then
flung into a filthy prison cell. As he lay there, his
captors taunted him, 'And now what of your plans
to evangelize the heathen?' Judson's reply was simple
and superb: 'My future is as bright as the promises of
God.'

Do you have the same kind of confidence in the
goodness of God and the faithfulness of his Word?
Are you serenely certain of God's overruling and care
when things go wrong? Are you absolutely convinced
that God will supply 'all your needs'? (Philippians
4:19.) Look at Psalm 23 again. Have you ever noticed
that David is not so much giving a word of testimony,
as making a statement of faith? What he says is that
'Goodness and love *will* follow me all the days of my
life.' He looks into a future that is unknown. He has
no idea what dangers, difficulties, hardships, pains and
problems may be there; but he is utterly convinced that
every day will be one in which he can depend upon the
unfailing goodness and love of his heavenly Shepherd.

Secondly, there is eternal security. Again, both our
passages take up this theme. In John 10, Jesus says of
his sheep, 'I give them eternal life, and they shall never
perish; no one can snatch them out of my hand. My
Father, who has given them to me, is greater than all;
no one can snatch them out of my Father's hand'
(John 10:28–29), while David ends Psalm 23 with the

triumphant assurance: 'And I will dwell in the house of the Lord for ever' (Psalm 23:6). In John 10, the Shepherd makes the promise; in Psalm 23 the sheep claims it! What a beautiful blending there is here — but are these passages intended to have any practical effect on our daily lives as Christians? Indeed they are, as are all the other truths we have examined in this study.

We noticed at the beginning of this chapter that there was not a single imperative, not one commandment or instruction, in either of the two main passages we are studying. All they did was to magnify the grace of God and show us his loving understanding of our needs. Let me remind you again of these points in a directly personal way.

Firstly, the Lord gave you *salvation*. By nature you did not want it, by self-effort you could not attain it and by self-instinct you did not know where to find it. You were blind and the Lord gave you sight, deaf and he opened your ears, sick and he made you whole, dead and he brought you to life.

He gave you then, and continues to give you now, *sensitivity* to his voice. He quickens your conscience, enabling you to sense with greater and greater clarity and certainty the things that will be a blessing to you and the things that will harm you. He opens the eyes of your understanding as you read the Bible, so that you have a supernatural knowledge of spiritual truth and can apply it to your daily life.

Then he sustains you, providing *all your spiritual needs,* lavishing upon you all that he has to give. He restores your soul, makes you lie down in green pastures, beside still waters. What is more, he satisfies you at the deepest point of your being, meeting the most profound longings of heart and spirit. He gives you life in all its fulness, so that your cup overflows.

Finally, he gives you *earthly and eternal security,*

promising that goodness and love will follow you all the days of your life and that you will dwell in the house of the Lord for ever, nothing or nobody being able to snatch you out of his hand.

But what about the commandments, the laws, the thunders and the lightnings? Where are the warnings, the exhortations, the disciplines, the demands? Of course, there are times when we do need to be sharply reminded of what Paul calls 'the sternness of God' (Romans 11:22) to jolt us out of sin, indiscipline, care-lessness or low-level living. But at other times God seeks to draw us closer to himself by a whispered revelation of his amazing love and unfailing promises.

That is what he is doing here. What are you doing?

4.

A Stone
Alive and welded

4.

A Stone
Alive and welded

Many of the titles given to Christians in the Bible are repeated again and again. This is certainly true of those at which we have looked so far — a son, a saint and a sheep. Now we turn to study a title that occurs only once, yet forms an important part of the biblical answer to our question: 'What in the world is a Christian?' The title concerned is 'a stone', and it occurs in the following passage from the First Epistle of Peter: 'As you come to him, the living Stone — rejected by men but chosen by God and precious to him — you also, *like living stones,* are being built into a spiritual house to be a holy priesthood, offering spiritual sacrifices acceptable to God through Jesus Christ' (1 Peter 2:5).

Peter tells us, then, that Christians are living stones, and although at first hearing this description hardly sounds very complimentary, nor seems to offer much potential for helpful development, we shall discover a great deal that is instructive, profitable and challenging as we take careful note of four basic truths contained in Peter's statement.

1. The transformation that is effected

There can surely be little doubt that it was the apostle Peter who wrote this particular letter. If you glance at the end of chapter 1 and the beginning of chapter 2 you will see a whole torrent of ideas and metaphors cascading over each other in just the kind of headlong language we would expect from such a man. What is even more fascinating is that it is Peter, of all people, who uses the word 'stones' as a description of Christians. When Peter was first brought to Jesus by his brother Andrew, we are told that Jesus looked at him and said, ' "You are Simon, son of John. You will be called Cephas" (which, when translated, is Peter)' (John 1:42). Oceans of ink have been spent in trying to get to the exact meaning of the precise words Jesus used here, but as this is not the primary passage we are studying, I am not going to add more than a few drops. What seems universally agreed is that the word 'Cephas' was originally the Aramaic *Kepha* and that its meaning is 'a rock' or 'rocky ground', something that spoke of stability. This new name was to replace the young disciple's natural name, Simon, and in so doing to give an indication of the supernatural change that was to take place in his life. Instead of being unstable and insecure, the new convert would become rock-solid, reliable, grounded in the faith.

Nor should we miss the prophetic element here. When he looked at Peter, Jesus saw not only into his face but into his heart and into his future. Notice the words: 'you are . . . you will be'. Jesus saw Peter as he was, and as he would become. He *saw* a blundering, impetuous, unstable fisherman; he *foresaw* Peter as a solid rock in the Christian faith. On that momentous day, Jesus not only gave Peter a new name, he gave him a new character.

We get the same picture elsewhere in Scripture. In the early part of the Old Testament, God says to Abram, 'No longer will you be called Abram; your name will be Abraham, for I have made you a father of many nations'

(Genesis 17:5). Some time later we have the story of Jacob's remarkable all-night encounter with a heavenly visitor, which ended with his being told, 'Your name will no longer be Jacob, but Israel, because you have struggled with God and with men and have overcome' (Genesis 32:28). In both of these cases, as with Peter, a change of name coincided with a change of nature, a change of dimension and a change of direction. A transformation was effected; the person concerned entered a new world.

So it is with the Chirstian, and surely the apostle Peter has this in mind when he describes Christians as 'living stones'. He may even be using the word 'living' to give his picture added emphasis. Certainly there is no more vivid way of describing the transforming experience of personal salvation than to say that the person concerned has 'crossed over from death to life' (John 5:24). We came across the same truth in the first of these studies, but we need to underline it in our thinking again and again so that we never forget the hopelessness of our condition outside of Christ, and the greatness and glory of our salvation. In the words of the apostle John, 'He who has the Son has life; he who does not have the Son of God does not have life' (1 John 5:12).

The great Renaissance sculptor Buonarroti Michelangelo was once working on a huge piece of rock when somebody asked him what he was doing. The rock seemed to have no shape or significance at all to the casual onlooker. Turning to his questioner, Michelangelo replied, 'I am releasing the angel that is imprisoned in this marble.' What a transformation there would be when the master's work was finished! Yet even this illustration does not begin to compare with what happens when a person becomes a Christian — because there is no angel in our human marble in the first place!

All the 'divine spark' theories, teaching as they do that every man is born with at least some small deposit of spiritual life that needs only to be cultivated, nurtured or developed, are so much unbiblical nonsense. Even David, one of the greatest men who ever lived, says plainly, 'Surely I have been a sinner from birth, sinful from the time my mother conceived me' (Psalm 51:5), while the apostle Paul identifies himself with all the rest of us when he says, 'We were by nature objects of wrath' (Ephesians 2:3). When a person becomes a Christian it is not because God applies a dose of heavenly hormones to our celestial embryo, but because, in a miracle beyond our understanding, he transforms us from being shapeless, useless, inanimate pieces of human fabric into what Peter graphically calls 'living stones'.

2. The integration that is required

Having described Christians as 'living stones', Peter goes on to say that they are 'being built into a spiritual house'. As Alan Stibbs comments, 'The phrase . . . implies that men enter the Church by coming to Christ, not that they become joined to Christ by entering the Church.' The point is well made, and exactly reflects what we are told about the growth of the early church, when 'the Lord added to their number daily those who were being saved' (Acts 2:47).

There is an extremely important lesson here. One of the current social fads is what we might call the 'drop-out philosophy'. People are dropping out of society, dropping out of school, dropping out of home, dropping out of their responsibilities to their fellow men. In the words of a modern theatrical production, their motto seems to be 'Stop the world, I want to get off!' Now I certainly sympathize with people who say, 'The world

seems to have gone mad. We've lost our corporate sense
of direction. This isn't the way things ought to be.'
I am inclined to agree with Vance Havner when he
says, 'Civilization is like an ape playing with matches in
a room full of dynamite'! But dropping out is not the
answer. If things are wrong, let us seek to put them
right. If society is insane, let us do whatever we can to
inject some sanity into it.

But these things are not only happening in the world,
they are also happening in the church. Some people,
and especially some young Christians who have pro-
fessed conversion in very informal circumstances or in
situations outside normal church activities are tempted
to opt out of the whole traditional church set-up. In a
restless urge to change things, or to get things done,
they try to bypass the traditional structures and organization of the church by 'going it alone', or by forming
small cells of like-minded people not answerable in any
way to a larger group. They turn their backs on the nor-
mally accepted church patterns and 'do their own
thing'. Now what do we say about this kind of situation?

Firstly, we must be careful not to issue a blanket
condemnation of all who do not associate themselves
with the ecclesiastical *status quo*. We have to recognize
that in some areas of our country there is no live church
for many miles. In other places the churches may be
icily unwelcoming to a newcomer who bursts on the
scene with what seems like irreverent enthusiasm —
the kind of place described by a friend of mine when
he said, 'It was so cold in there I could have skated down
the aisles!' Again, there are young couples living on
housing estates too far removed from an evangelical
church to make attendance there a reasonable possibility. In cases like these, who will lift the first stone
to throw at those who, having prayed carefully about

the situation, begin to conduct Sunday worship in a home, or join with others to meet in a very 'unestablished' way in some 'secular' building? Few things excite me more than modern stories of thriving churches which began in exactly this kind of way.

But the one thing that must be avoided assiduously is Christian *isolationism,* carrying the drop-out philosophy into our Christian experience. The Bible speaks not of dropping out but of being 'built into a spiritual house'. The writer to the Hebrews is quite specific on this point, when he says, 'Let us not give up meeting together, as some are in the habit of doing' (Hebrews 10:25). Of course, the church is far from perfect. Of course, it makes mistakes. Of course, it has its anachronisms, inconsistencies and hypocrisies. But you will not change any of these things by leaving the church, or by refusing to meet with other Christians and instead setting up shop on your own! A thousand bricks lying scattered over a building site are of little value. Nobody doubts that they are bricks, but their potential is not realized until they are cemented together with other bricks and built into something that can give protection, comfort, storage or a place in which work can be done. Only as part of a building with order, shape and purpose is a brick of real value. As Frank Colquhoun says, 'As far as the New Testament is concerned, there is no such thing as a churchless Christianity. The church is not a burdensome appendage to the Christian religion; it *is* the Christian religion in its organized form and outward manifestation.'

No Christian can forward the kingdom of God better by standing aloof from other Christians like a solitary brick on a building site. Get involved in your local church! Get involved in its programme, its ministry, its prayer life, its burdens, its responsibilities, its fellowship. Only then will you be involved in its blessings.

3. The identification that is suggested

So far, our study has centered entirely on the fact
that *Christians* are described as 'living stones'. But
it is also important to notice that in this passage Peter
also describes *Christ* as 'the living Stone'. He repeats
the description a moment later, calling him 'a chosen
and precious cornerstone' (1 Peter 2:6). He is quoting
here from the Old Testament, where God says, 'See,
I lay . . . in Zion a tested stone, a precious cornerstone
for a sure foundation' (Isaiah 28:16).

Of the many truths that flow from the picture of
Jesus as a 'stone', let us concentrate on just one that
fits perfectly into our present study. The simplest way
to put it is that in being given the same title or name as
Christ, Christians can be said to be identified with him.
Some years ago I was leading a houseparty in Norway,
and we were having a marvellous time, exploring God's
Word and God's world. One day it rained so hard and
for so long that we were confined to our hotel for over
twenty-four hours. After the obligatory postcards had
all been written, people gathered around in informal
groups to pass the time away. Some played table games,
others read books. But one group decided to do something else. They took a large sheet of paper, wrote a
long word at the top of it, then spent several hours
seeing how many other words they could make, using
only the letters of their original word. If I remember
correctly, they ended up with over 200. And the word
with which they began? 'Identification'. It was remarkable what they got out of that single word, and it is
remarkable how much truth flows from the biblical doctrine that the Christian is identified with Christ.

For instance, at the end of Colossians 2 and the
beginning of Colossians 3 we find these four phrases
grouped closely together: 'You died with Christ' (2:20);

'You have been raised with Christ' (3:1); 'Your life is now hidden with Christ in God' (3:3); and 'You also will appear with him in glory' (3:4). Taking all these phrases together, the Christian is seen to be identified with Christ in his rejection, his resurrection, his reign and his return. To put it the other way round, everything that Jesus was and is, everything that Jesus did and does, is linked in with the life of the Christian. The life, death, resurrection, reign and return of Christ are for the blessing and benefit of his people. Christ was rejected by the world; so is the Christian. Christ rose from the dead; we, too, have been raised to newness of life. Christ reigns in glory, and by means of his grace we can lay hold of his reigning power to triumph over all our earthly circumstances. Christ will return to the earth in majesty and great glory, and we shall be taken to be with him for ever.

Yet this great truth about the Christian's identification with Christ carries with it the obvious responsibility to live in such a way that people can *recognize* our identification in practical terms. Someone once put it in the form of a question: 'If you were arrested on a charge of being a Christian, would there be enough evidence to convict you?' Imagine yourself in a court of law, charged with being a follower of Christ. Now think of the people who might be called to give evidence: your husband or wife, your parents or children, your boy friend or girl friend, your boss or your employees, your fellow students, the other members of your sports club, your customers, your clients, the minister of your church. The list is endless — and the possibilities unnerving! Now when they had all given their evidence of what they knew of your life, would an honest judge convict you? I am afraid that some professing Christians would be acquitted on the spot, with costs against the prosecution!

The other obvious point about identification is that

we should never be ashamed of being identified with
Christ. Some people are perfectly happy about being
identified with a particular church or denomination or
theological school of thought, but somehow they feel
embarrassed at being identified in a personal way with
Christ. Yet our identification is essentially with *him,* not
primarily with an organization. A Christian was once
asked, 'Don't you belong to the Methodist Church?'
to which he replied, 'No, I am a member of the Methodist Church, but I *belong* to Jesus Christ.' No Christian
should be ashamed of declaring his allegiance to Christ.
To say with Peter under pressure, 'I don't know the
man!' (Matthew 26:72), even when we say it by our
silence, is an act of shameful betrayal. I remember once
seeing a Muslim take out his prayer mat in the middle
of Athens Airport and, apparently oblivious of the hundreds of other passengers thronging that sophisticated,
commercial, secular building, go through his routine of
prayer and worship, bowing in the direction of Mecca,
his feet bare, his forehead touching the ground. Now I
am not suggesting that it would be a good thing for
Christians to make a public display of their private worship in the middle of the Departure Lounge at Heath-
row! But I must say that that unenlightened man spoke
deeply to my own heart about my willingness to be
identified openly with my Lord and Saviour in today's
world.

4. The oblations that are desired

Having spoken of Christians as 'living stones' and of
their integration into the spiritual house of the church,
Peter goes on to say that this is in order to be 'a holy
priesthood, offering spiritual sacrifices acceptable to
God through Jesus Christ'. In his typically breathless

style he runs one idea into another with bewildering speed. He speaks of Christians as stones and sees them as parts of a building, and at the same time says that they are priests and should be offering sacrifices. Now in the natural world there is a vast difference between the building and the people who occupy it, but the Bible is so rich and diverse in its descriptions of Christians that Peter can see us as both. Christians not only form the building, they do so in order to carry out the purpose for which the building is erected, and that purpose, says Peter, is to offer up 'spiritual sacrifices acceptable to God through Jesus Christ'.

In the Old Testament, sacrifices were clearly an important part of worship. A special building was set aside for the purpose and certain people were carefully selected to perform the sacred duties of priests on behalf of the others. Specific animals were taken and sacrificed according to minutely detailed regulations. This is the background to Peter's picture, which contrasts so sharply with it. The emphasis under the New Covenant is not on a building but on the people. *They* form the church. Then the sacrifices are not to be offered by a select few, but by all, for every Christian is said to be a priest. Finally, the offerings are not animals, but what Peter calls 'spiritual sacrifices'. These are the oblations that God desires.

But what are these 'spiritual sacrifices'? It would be fairly easy to invent a neatly parcelled list of things that would be 'acceptable to God' in our lives, but let us keep precisely to Scripture and list things specifically mentioned there as being spiritual sacrifices that are pleasing to him.

Firstly, there is sorrow for sin. In his great penitential psalm David says, 'The sacrifices of God are a broken spirit; a broken and contrite heart, O God, you will not despise' (Psalm 51:17). Here is the first of these spiritual sacrifices which God requires from us as his people. When the Holy Spirit reveals something in our lives that grieves him we should turn to the Lord with broken and contrite hearts. Can you remember when you last shed a genuine tear because of sin in your life? Do you know what it is to be genuinely ashamed or broken-hearted because of your behaviour, your language, your pride, your envy, your greed, your coldness of heart, the meanness of your giving, the poverty of your worship, your reluctance to witness or any other failure in your life? Philip Henry once wrote, 'You should never think of sin without repenting.' Sorrow for sin is a sacrifice which God rightly demands of us, and one in which he always meets us in blessing.

Secondly, there is the ministry of money. In his letter to the Philippians, Paul thanks them for certain gifts they had made towards his ministry, and goes on to assure them, 'I am amply supplied, now that I have received from Epaphroditus the gifts you sent. They are a fragrant offering, an acceptable sacrifice, pleasing to God' (Philippians 4:18). When we speak about sacrificial giving we are usually thinking about the amount of the gift or its cost to the giver, but in this passage Paul is speaking about the spirit in which the gift was made and its acceptability in the sight of God. To sense whether our giving is a sacrifice 'pleasing to God' we must assess it not merely in terms of amount, but of the spirit of the gift, of our willingness to give.

Robert Rodenmayer has said that there are three kinds of giving: grudge giving, duty giving and thanksgiving. Grudge giving says, 'I have to'; duty giving says, 'I ought to'; thanksgiving says, 'I want to'. Which of these do you honestly think is the closest to describing the spirit of your giving to Christian work? Perhaps a frivolous story will help to make my point. A boy was once given a 50p piece and a 10p piece by his father and told to put into the offering plate at church that day whichever coin he felt was right in the light of what the Bible taught about giving. After the service, the boy returned the 50p piece to his father. Naturally disappointed, he asked the boy why he had felt it right to give the smaller coin in the offering. 'Because', junior replied, 'the Bible says, "God loves a cheerful giver" and I was much more cheerful giving 10p than I would have been giving 50p!' The story may be trivial, but a trickle of truth seeps through. The Bible *does* say, 'God loves a cheerful giver' (2 Corinthians 9:7) and the Greek word for 'cheerful' is *hilaros,* the basis of our English word 'hilarious'. Generous giving to the Lord should be the constant delight of every Christian. Does this say anything about the spirit in which you exercise the ministry of giving? Do you give in a way that makes your gifts 'an acceptable sacrifice, pleasing to God'?

Thirdly, there is praise and thanksgiving. Coming towards the end of the Epistle to the Hebrews, the writer makes the following exhortation: 'Through Jesus, therefore, let us continually offer to God a sacrifice of praise – the fruit of lips that confess his name' (Hebrews 13:15). Here is another of the 'spiritual sacrifices' to which Peter is referring in the passage we are studying – and perhaps it is one that is often sadly missing in the lives of Christians today. Back in the sixteenth century, George Herbert penned these words: 'O Thou who hast given us so much, mercifully grant us one thing more, a grateful heart.' We need to pray that prayer often! The Bible teaches that one of the marks of the Spirit-filled Christian is that he is 'always giving thanks to God the Father for everything, in the name of our Lord Jesus Christ' (Ephesians 5:20). Elsewhere, he tells the Thessalonians to 'give thanks in all circumstances, for this is God's will for you in Christ Jesus' (1 Thessalonians 5:18).

Yet this is far from easy. It is obviously easy to give thanks to God when everything is going well, when the sky is blue and the sea is calm; when everything is harmonious at home and prosperous at work; when our health is good and when the Lord is obviously blessing our Christian service. But what happens when difficulties arise and problems multiply and the pressures mount? Is it not true that thanksgiving is one of the first things to disappear, or at least to begin to evaporate? Preaching on the text, 'But the fruit of the Spirit is . . . joy' (Galatians 5:22), C.H. Spurgeon once said, 'Brethren, if we ever become perfect in heart, *we shall joy in all the divine will,* whatever it may bring us. I am trying, if I can, to find joy in rheumatism, but I cannot get up to it yet. I have found a joy when it is over — I can reach that length — and I can and do bless God for any good result that may come from it; but when the pain is on me, it is difficult to be joyous about it, and so I conclude that my sanctification is very incomplete, and my conformity to the divine will is sadly imperfect.' There spoke an honest man! Let us continually ask God to give us a grateful heart, whatever he allows or directs to come into our lives.

Fourthly, there is doing good by sharing.   In the very next sentence to the one at which we have been looking, the writer to the Hebrews says, 'And do not forget to do good and to share with others, for with such sacrifices God is pleased' (Hebrews 13:16). When people speak about a 'do-gooder' in these days they sometimes mean it in a somewhat cynical way. They have in mind a rather spineless, characterless individual helping lame dogs over stiles, or they think of some tweedy Amazon rattling a collection box in the High Street. But in the Bible a 'do-gooder' is invested with all the dignity of deity, for it is said of the Lord Jesus himself that 'he went around doing good' (Acts 10:38). Nobody need be ashamed of a spirit which draws them to invest their time and talents in helping their fellow men and sharing with them the good things God has given to them.

Of course, the good things that can be shared with others in the spirit of the passage in Hebrews are endless. Some commentators think the writer has the gospel in mind, but in my view this is limiting the command in a quite arbitrary and unbiblical way. Many more down-to-earth things come to mind. The couple with room to spare can offer the freedom of their home to a student looking for digs; the comparatively well-to-do businessman has a better opportunity for substantial giving than others; the tradesman can occasionally make his particular goods or services available freely or cheaply to people in genuine need; the housewife with grown-up children off her hands can use her new free time to help the sick, the elderly, the handicapped or the over-stressed.

In a nutshell, Christians should be the finest neighbours people have and the most generous, helpful, open-hearted members of the social circles in which they move. To expand the issue to the wider horizons of need which the Christian should help to meet would be to run out of space to mention them, but we could begin with the *millions* of our fellow human beings who will spend today below starvation level. To this whole area, the Bible speaks quite explicitly: 'Therefore, as we have opportunity, let us do good to all people, especially to those who belong to the family of believers' (Galatians 6:10). By doing so, we contribute to the divinely ordained way of carrying out God's loving and merciful purposes in the world.

There is a well-known story of a London church badly damaged during an air raid in World War II. In the process of restoring it for worship, it was found that a statue of Christ had been shattered to pieces.

Somebody carefully put it together again, but found that both hands were missing. It stayed like that for some time, looking not only incomplete but somehow pointless. Then somebody attached a card to it on which these words were written: 'Christ has no hands but our hands to do his work today.' Think through the essential truth of those words, and show by the consistency of your 'spiritual sacrifices' that you are a vital part of God's 'spiritual house'!

5.

A Soldier
On active service

5.

A Soldier
On active service

Consider these two pictures. In the first, a group of men, women and children are strolling slowly through a country churchyard on a Sunday morning, with the sun shining and the air filled with the mingled melodies of church bells and bird-song. In the second, a hopelessly outnumbered group of soldiers, completely surrounded by a ruthless and hideous enemy bent on massacre, try to fight their way through a blood-drenched battlefield.

It would be difficult to imagine two more totally different pictures, yet when we open the pages of the Bible we find that they synchronize in yet another scriptural definition of a Christian, and that is that a Christian is a soldier. Paul's letter to Timothy alone would be sufficient for us to discover that. He writes, 'Timothy, my son, I give you this instruction in keeping with the prophecies once made about you, so that by following them you may fight the good fight' (1 Timothy 1:18). Towards the end of this letter, he urges him, 'Fight the good fight of the faith' (1 Timothy 6:12). In his second letter to Timothy, he tells him to 'endure hardship with us like a good soldier of Christ Jesus' (2 Timothy 2:3).

This picture of the Christian as a soldier, and of the church as an army, has been the inspiration of many of our best-known hymns such as 'Onward Christian soldiers', 'Fight the good fight', 'Sound the battle-cry',

'Soldiers of Christ arise' and so on. The same theme comes through in the Book of Common Prayer. In the service of Holy Communion laid down there, there is a point where the minister has an opportunity to mention special items for prayer. These may be international, social, local, matters concerning individual people in the church, and so on. But whatever these 'biddings' may be, they always end with the words: 'And let us pray for the whole state of Christ's church *militant* here on earth.' Hymn-books and church manuals combine, then, to take up this great biblical theme: a Christian is a soldier. In this study we shall look briefly at three aspects of this truth.

1. The Christian soldier's opposition.

Corrie Ten Boom has said that 'The first step on the way to victory is to recognize the enemy' and that is certainly true in the realm of Christian warfare. With an open Bible before him, no Christian should have a great deal of difficulty in doing that, and as we consider the nature of the opposition we face we can certainly say these three things about it.

Firstly, it is diabolical. In other words it is satanic; it is led, master-minded and planned by the devil, and carried out by him and by the unseen hosts of evil at his disposal. Now for some people, a statement like that belongs to the realm of fantasy. They simply do not believe that there is such a person or power as the devil. A survey carried out in Britain in 1969 revealed that only 21% of the population believed in the devil's existence. Dr Charles Malik, former President of the United Nations General Assembly, was right when he declared, 'We have lost the sense of the eternal battle raging between Christ and the devil.'

But no Christian has any excuse for making that terrible mistake. The Bible describes the devil as a living person and the implacable enemy of God and the Christian. Jesus likened him to 'a strong man, fully armed' (Luke 11:21) and called him 'the prince of this world' (John 14:30). Paul called him 'the god of this age' (2 Corinthians 4:4) and 'the ruler of the kingdom of the air' (Ephesians 2:2). Peter wrote of him that he 'prowls around like a roaring lion looking for someone to devour' (1 Peter 5:8) and John named him 'the angel of the Abyss' (Revelation 9:11). The cartoonist's caricature of the devil as a red-faced old man with pointed ears, a toasting-fork in his hand and his tail sticking out of his trousers is no more than that — a caricature. The Bible teaches that he is a living super-power, an evil genius, unspeakably cruel, incredibly cunning and powerful beyond all human imagination.

This is confirmed by examining his track record. When Adam and Eve were lured into sin, it was the devil's deadly work; when Job was tempted to turn his back on God, it was as the direct result of the devil's activities; when Judas Iscariot betrayed Jesus to the authorities at Jerusalem we are told that 'Satan entered into him' (John 13:27); when Paul explained to the Christians at Thessalonica why he had not been able to carry out his evangelistic plans he said plainly, 'Satan stopped us' (1 Thessalonians 2:18). In these widely differing situations one underlying theme remains constant: the devil was at work, defiling, degrading, defying, defeating. Taken together, they should teach us that no area of life is safe from him and no avenue of approach closed to him. He attacks along all the fronts of our lives and personalities.

He attacks physically. Paul says that his 'thorn in [his] flesh' (nobody seems clear as to the precise nature of this, but it is generally agreed that it was some kind of

physical trouble) was 'a messenger of Satan, to torment
me' (2 Corinthians 12:7). A crippled woman was said
by Jesus to be someone 'whom Satan has kept bound
for eighteen long years' (Luke 13:16). There is no suggestion in either of these cases that all physical illness
is the direct result of sin, but it is equally obvious that
the physical realm is one in which the devil has scope
and power to operate.

He attacks mentally.   Paul tells the Corinthians that
Satan has 'blinded the minds of unbelievers, so that they
cannot see the light of the gospel of the glory of Christ'
(2 Corinthians 4:4) and later in the same letter warns
his readers that 'just as Eve was deceived by the serpent's
cunning, your minds may somehow be led astray from
your sincere and pure devotion to Christ' (2 Corinthians
11:3). His power to distort men's mental processes is
underlined by Christ's description of him as 'a liar and
the father of lies' (John 8:44). It is a major part of his
ministry of deceit to warp, bend, twist, pollute and con-
fuse man's mental processes, and beyond that to bring
about the disorientation, despair and depression that
so often follow.

He attacks spiritually.   When Ananias and his wife
deceived the early church over the selling price of their
land, Peter challenged him, 'Ananias, how is it that
Satan has so filled your heart that you have lied to the
Holy Spirit and have kept for yourself some of the
money you received for the land?' (Acts 5:3.) I have
deliberately chosen this one incident to show that even in
the most common of sins, dishonesty, man is suffering
defeat at the hands of the devil, who attacks in the
realm of the heart, the will, the conscience, the desire.

Here, then, is the first thing we must recognize about
the opposition we face as Christians. It is diabolical.
The Christian life is not a ball, it is a battlefield, and the
enemy is none other than Satan himself.

Secondly, it is spiritual. This follows from the fact
that our opponent is a spiritual and not a physical being.
In Paul's words, 'Our struggle is not against flesh and
blood, but against the rulers, against the authorities,
against the powers of this dark world and against the
spiritual forces of evil in the heavenly realms' (Ephesians
6:12). The opposition the Christian faces is not basically
outward and physical, but inward and spiritual. It does
have outward, physical and visible manifestations, of
course, for example in the areas of materialism and the
misuse of sex, but these only reflect principles that are
inward and spiritual. The conflicts and issues of life are
matters of the mind, the will, the heart, the conscience
and the spirit. Jesus brought this out very clearly in
this piece of teaching: 'Don't you see that nothing that
enters a man from the outside can make him "unclean"?
For it doesn't go into his heart but into his stomach,
and then out of his body' (In saying this, Jesus declared
all foods 'clean'). He went on: 'What comes out of
a man is what makes him 'unclean'. For from within,
out of men's hearts, come evil thoughts, sexual immorality, theft, murder, adultery, greed, malice, deceit, lewd-
ness, envy, slander, arrogance and folly. All these evils
come from inside and make a man "unclean" ' (Mark
7:18–23).

Nothing could be clearer. The Christian soldier's
battle is not physical but spiritual. If you could shut
yourself away from all outward temptation, you would
still find yourself caught up in a spiritual warfare. The
real battlefield is not on your eyeballs, nor on the surface of your skin, but in the treacherous depths of your
human nature. The opposition is spiritual!

Thirdly, it is personal. This is obvious, but let us make
the point. While taking part in a conference in West
Germany, I had a meal with a German and a Dutchman.
Both Christians, they began to share stories about World

War II. It transpired that they were fighting in the same area of northern Europe at the same time — though, of course, on opposite sides. As they filled in more and more details of their experiences, they came to the conclusion that on one particular day they must have been within a matter of yards of each other during several hours of bitter hand-to-hand fighting for the possession of one particular village. During those hours they had been doing their utmost to kill each other, yet their opposition was in no way personal. They did not know each other. The battle they were fighting was one of political and nationalistic forces. It was a battle of ideologies, not personalities.

I give the illustration by way of contrast, because in the Christian warfare the conflict is intensely personal. When there were only two human beings on the face of the earth, the devil fought them one at a time. So today, with a detailed dossier on our circumstances, our background, our temperament and our weaknesses, he tempts, attacks and fights us as individuals. One has only to read the experiences of New Testament Christians to see them singled out for attack in order to achieve victories of wider significance. This truth brings with it a very important lesson. You cannot ultimately escape in the crowd, or shelter under the umbrella of the church, or register as a conscientious objector in today's spiritual warfare. Every Christian is a soldier. Every Christian is in the battle. Every Christian faces diabolical, spiritual and personal opposition.

2. The Christian soldier's objectives

Having seen something of the opposition we face as Christians in today's world, what should be our objectives? I remember Major Bill Batt — a distinguished soldier and effective Christian — once telling me, 'Maintenance of the objective was the first rule of war I was ever taught,' and I have never forgotten his words. Whatever the circumstances, a soldier must remember the object of the exercise in which he is engaged, and always keep it in the forefront of his thinking, straining every sinew to fulfil it to the best of his ability, regardless of the cost to himself. I remember reading an American serviceman's description of a Japanese kamikaze attack on his ship, in which he said, 'We saw him coming out of the sun, heading for our ship. We tried desperately to stop him, but he got through our flak and struck the deck and bounced and came to a stop. The bomb was a dud. We opened the cockpit and found a fifteen-year-old Japanese, still alive, *chained inside.*' This young fighter, no more than a teenager, was so committed to his cause, that he was prepared to maintain his objective even at what he believed to be the certain cost of his own life. In ways that may be less dramatic, but should be no less positive, the Christian soldier is called upon to discipline himself to maintain life's spiritual objectives. What are they?

Firstly, the enemy's withdrawal. Two Christian friends who share my deep interest in Czechoslovakia once told me of their reaction when the Warsaw Pact countries invaded it in 1968. 'This is God's country', they told me, 'and the devil has taken it over. We are going to do everything we can to push him back by taking the gospel there.' Their statement was idealistic, dramatic but, of course, not strictly true. Czechoslovakia is no more God's country than the countries that combined to invade it in such a shameful way. Nor would the withdrawal of all Communist influence automatically produce a Christian revival in the country. But I understood what they were saying, and their vivid language helps to illustrate the objective that should be firmly in the

heart of every Christian. The prophet Isaiah writes,
'But now, this is what the Lord says — he who created
you, O Jacob, he who formed you, O Israel: "Fear not,
for I have redeemed you; I have called you by my name;
you are mine" ' (Isaiah 43:1). As we face the devil's
attacks, we need to keep this firmly in mind. God has
created and redeemed us. He calls us his own. Everything we are and have belongs to him. The devil has no
right to our eyes, our feet, our hands, our bodies, our
minds, our time or our talents. All of these belong to
God and are exclusively *his*. The Christian's philosophy
of battle ought therefore to include a determination to
repel every attempt of the devil to occupy God's terri-
tory.

But let us be careful here, and not fall into a subtle
trap. We will never succeed in destroying the devil. Nor
can we reach a situation where we have got rid of his
influence for the rest of our lives. There is no such thing
in genuine Christian experience as a once-for-all dramatic crisis that gets rid of the process of fighting the
devil throughout our lives. When Jesus was tempted
in the wilderness he faced and repelled three attacks
by the devil. But we read that, 'When the devil had
finished all this tempting, he left him *until an oppor-
tune time*' (Luke 4:13). These were neither the first
nor the last times that Jesus faced the fierce attacks of
the devil. He continued to be tempted and attacked
throughout his earthly life, the Bible describing him as
having been 'tempted in every way, just as we are'
(Hebrews 4:15). The temptation in the wilderness was
not a once-for-all crisis, it was merely a highlight in a
lifelong battle.

We too face a lifelong battle. The devil will attack
repeatedly, choosing his method and moment with unnerving cunning. Yet as often as he attacks, so often are
we to aim at his withdrawal. By prayer, faith, discipline,

Christian fellowship and the Word of God, we are to aim at the fulfilment of the promise given to us: 'Submit yourselves, then, to God. Resist the devil, and he will flee from you' (James 4:7). The devil's withdrawal is one clear objective the Christian must have.

Secondly, the Lord's approval.   Paul puts it like this: 'No one serving as a soldier gets involved in civilian affairs — *he wants to please his commanding officer*' (2 Timothy 2:4). The life of Jesus certainly personified that principle. He told those arguing about his mission in the world that as the Son of Man he was acting under his heavenly Father's authority, adding, 'I always do *what pleases him*' (John 8:29). The same theme runs right through the Bible. Writing to Christians in Greece about the ministry of evangelism, Paul said, 'We are *not trying to please men but God,* who tests our hearts' (1 Thessalonians 2:4). Moving on to encourage them to live godly lives, he gives them this motive: 'Finally brothers, we instructed you how to live *in order to please God,* as in fact you are living. Now we ask you and urge you in the Lord Jesus to do this more and more' (1 Thessalonians 4:1). The writer of the Epistle to the Hebrews said of Enoch that 'Before he was taken, he was commended *as one who pleased God*' (Hebrews 11:5). John linked consistent answers to prayer with the fact that 'we obey [God's] commands *and do what pleases him*' (1 John 3:22).

All of this scriptural material underlines an important truth about the Christian life, and that is that being a Christian is not a matter of rules and regulations, quotas and ratios, mathematics and percentages. Nowhere, for instance, are we told to aim at a certain 'percentage of purity'. Basically, the Christian life is a matter of relationship to the Lord. It is not a matter of passing some clinical examination, but of seeking in all things to 'do what pleases him'.

A soldier: on active service   91

These, then, are the twin objectives of the Christian
soldier's life — the enemy's withdrawal and the Lord's
approval. In other words, we should always aim to be
looking at the Lord's face and the devil's back. Happy
the Christian who is becoming increasingly familiar
with those two views!

3. The Christian soldier's optimism

During World War I, the French leader Field Marshal
Foch sent this famous message to General Joffre: 'My
right is broken, my left is shattered, my centre is in re-
treat. The situation is excellent; let us attack!' That
must have sounded like either insanity or super-optimism
to the soldiers who had to carry out his orders, and it
may sound equally remarkable to speak of the Christian
soldier's optimism in the light of all we have seen of
the devil's tremendous power. Yet the Christian soldier
can enter every day of his spiritual warfare with genuine
optimism and with the confidence that he can emerge
victorious, and we will close this study by looking at
three reasons why this is so.
Firstly, because God's provisions are available. The
classic biblical passage on Christian warfare is Ephesians
6, where Paul not only speaks about the Christian's
enemies but also lists the equipment available to him
for the contest. Having left his readers under no illusions
about the reality and power of the forces opposing them,
he then gives them these battle orders: 'Therefore put
on the full armour of God, so that when the day of evil
comes, you may be able to stand your ground, and
after you have done everything, to stand. Stand firm
then, with the belt of truth buckled around your waist,
with the breastplate of righteousness in place, and with
your feet fitted with the readiness that comes from the

gospel of peace. In addition to all this, take up the shield
of faith, with which you can extinguish all the flaming
arrows of the evil one. Take the helmet of salvation and
the sword of the Spirit, which is the word of God. And
pray in the Spirit on all occasions with all kinds of
prayers and requests' (Ephesians 6:13—18).

Each of the items Paul mentions here deserves a detailed study on its own — one which in this brief look
we are unable to give — but the essential point to be
made is that they form part of God's provision for
the Christian soldier. What is more, because God has
provided them, they must be effective. When a Christian
loses a battle it is always because he has not rightly
used the equipment that God has provided for his defence and protection. If you want to be an effective
soldier of Christ, make a serious study of Ephesians 6,
and learn how to put your battledress on.

Secondly, because God's promises are accessible.   In
the seventeenth century a Church of England minister
by the name of William Gurnall wrote a classic book on
Ephesians 6:10—17. In its original form the book ran
to 877 pages, but the modern version condenses it to
a mere 603! In what we would now call the Foreword
to the book — but then called 'The Epistles Dedicatory'
— Gurnall wrote, in the quaint language of his time,
'Whet your courage at the throne of grace, from whence
all your recruits of soul-strength come. *Send faith oft
up the hill of promise,* to see and bring you the certain
news of Christ's coming to you, yea, and assured victory
with him.' Quaint it may be, but it is right on line! The
Christian soldier can fight with confidence because of
the many promises that are his in God's Word. Let me
remind you of two, one as it were for every day, and
one for life's battle as a whole.

The first is one we have already noticed, where James
says, 'Submit yourselves, then, to God. Resist the devil,

and he will flee from you' (James 4:7). Now that is a
promise! He will not flee for good. He will not leave
you unmolested in the future. But God has promised
that the devil's attacks *can* be turned back, and we
ought to take God at his word and look in faith for the
promise to be fulfilled. The second promise is where
Paul writes, 'I have fought the good fight, I have finished
the race, I have kept the faith. Now there is in store for
me the crown of righteousness, which the Lord, the
righteous Judge, will award to me on that day — and not
only to me, but also to all who have longed for his
appearing' (2 Timothy 4:7–8). Now that is another
promise! The day is coming when the war will be over,
the last attack spent, the last temptation finished, the
last pressure lifted; and when that happens you will
stand secure in God's eternal presence wearing what
Paul calls 'the crown of righteousness'. How confidently
would an athlete run if he knew he was going to win
the race? How confidently would a soldier fight if he
was certain that his enemy would lie defeated at the
end of the day? Then how should we as Christians
face the battles, trials, temptations and pressures of our
earthly life? Surely we should do so with confidence.

Thirdly, because God's presence is assured.   Everybody
knows the Old Testament story of David and Goliath.
When these two stood face to kneecaps in front of the
Philistines and the Israelites, any fair-minded boxing
official would have declared it 'No Contest'. Goliath
was 9 feet 9 inches tall. He had a coat of armour weigh-
ing 12 stone. The head of his spear tipped the scales at
12 lbs. All David seemed to be able to offer was a crude
sling, five stones and a suntan! But when Goliath had
finished his arrogant ranting, David looked at him
calmly and said this: 'You come against me with sword
and spear and javelin, but I come against you in the
name of the Lord Almighty, the God of the armies of

Israel, whom you have defied. This day the Lord will
hand you over to me . . . for the battle is the Lord's,
and he will give all of you into our hands' (1 Samuel
17:45—47). David was expressing his unflinching faith
in one decisive factor — that God was fighting on his
side. Anything he would do in the coming battle would
not be in his own human strength, but in the power of
the living God. No wonder he was confident — and the
same confidence, for the same reason, is restated again
and again in Scripture. The psalmist says, 'Through you
we push back our enemies; *through your name* we
trample our foes' (Psalm 44:5); Paul writes, 'For though
we live in the world, we do not wage war as the world
does. The weapons we fight with are not the weapons
of the world. On the contrary, they have *divine power*
to demolish strongholds' (2 Corinthians 10:3—4). He
tells the Romans that in all of life's battles 'we are more
than conquerors *through him* who loved us' (Romans
8:37) and even dares to say to the Philippians, 'I can do
everything *through him* who gives me strength' (Philippians 4:13).

Here is the open secret of the Christian's confidence
in the battle of life. The Christian soldier is called upon
to watch, fight, pray, resist, struggle, be disciplined,
wrestle, strive. These are his inescapable responsibilities.
*But he is never called upon to do these things in his own
strength*. He is to be 'strong *in the Lord* and in *his*
mighty power' (Ephesians 6:10). In ordinary warfare,
the strength of a general lies in that of his troops. In our
spiritual warfare the strength of the troops lies in the
power of their heavenly General. William Gurnall has it
absolutely right here, too: 'Take heart, therefore, O ye
saints, and be strong; your cause is good, God himself
espouseth your quarrel, who hath appointed you his
own Son, General of the field, called "Captain of our
salvation". He shall lead you on with courage, and

bring you off with honour. He lived and died for you; he will live and die with you; for mercy and tenderness to his soldiers, none like him . . . For success insuperable; he never lost a battle even when he lost his life; he won in the field, carrying the spoils thereof in the triumphant chariot of his ascension, to heaven with him, where he makes an open show of them to the unspeakable joy of saints and angels.'

Onward Christian soldiers!

6.

A Steward
The inescapable duty

6.

A Steward
The inescapable duty

Among the many books in my study, one of the most battered is an old etymological dictionary. Etymology is the study of the origins of words and I find it endlessly fascinating to discover exactly how words we commonly use today came into being. Our English language is one of the richest in the world, mainly because we have plundered Greek, Latin, French, German and countless other tongues to form our own.

Take the very ordinary word 'steward', for instance. How would you explain it in a simplified dictionary? It is not easy to condense into one brief phrase all the ideas that come to mind, but let us look at the etymology and see what we find. The word comes from the Middle English 'stiward' and the Anglo-Saxon 'stiweard'. The 'sti' part is a shortened form of the ancient word 'stig' or 'stiga', which probably meant 'a house' (the nearest word we have from this root today is the word 'sty'), while the 'weard' part has now become 'ward' (to guard or take care of). Putting all that together, we would have something like 'to take care of a house or property'.

All very fascinating, but does it have anything to do with our present series of studies? Yes it does, because one of the New Testament definitions of a Christian is that he is a *steward*. Having said that, we need to dig just a little deeper, because New Testament Greek has its own etymology and our English word 'steward' as it appears in Scripture translates the Greek word *oikonomos,* which in turn is made up of two separate words. The first is *oikos,* which means 'a house' and the second is the verb *nemo,* 'to arrange'. By placing the two strands of etymology together we can now see that technically speaking a steward is the arranger or manager of a house or property. In modern usage, he might be someone put in charge of an estate, for instance, usually in the absence of the owner. The word is also used of an official with responsibility for organizing a race meeting, or even of someone serving drinks behind a bar, but the sense remains basically the same: a steward is in charge of property belonging to someone else.

Here endeth the etymological lesson! However, it will all prove helpful as we study three aspects of the biblical statement that a Christian is a steward.

1. The responsibility of Christian stewardship

It will already be obvious that the very concept of stewardship implies responsibility, whether the properties or matters concerned are large or small. Responsibility is of the very essence of stewardship; indeed, the two terms are almost synonymous. This comes across in the opening words of a parable Jesus told: 'There was a rich man whose manager was accused of wasting his possessions. So he called him in and asked him, "What is this I hear about you? Give an account of your management..." ' (Luke 16:1–2). The word translated 'manager' is the Greek *oikonomos* and even this brief snatch of Scripture captures the spirit of the word. The servant concerned was *responsible.* The same spirit comes across in something Jesus said earlier, when he spoke of a 'faithful and wise manager (*oikonomos*), whom the master puts in charge of his servants' (Luke 12:42). Here again, what comes through loud and clear is the sense of *responsibility*. What is more, it was a two-sided responsibility; the steward or manager was responsible *to* his master and *for* his master's business. He was not his own boss. The goods he managed were not his own. Everything that passed through his hands belonged to the one who had placed him in that position.

What a clear lesson this already has to teach us with regard to our position as Christians! The unconverted man never thinks in these terms. Life, goods, time, talent — he thinks of all these things as being *his*. But to think like this is to run clean contrary to God's economy. As Warran Quanbeck puts it in his book *Stewardship in Contemporary Theology,* 'Man is most truly himself, not when he struts about in pride of ability and possession, but when he sees himself as a creature of God and submits to the will of his Creator which is his true happiness.' The roots of biblical stewardship, then, lie in a right understanding of the Christian's relationship to the Lord, and nowhere is this more clearly put than in these words by Paul: 'You are not your own; you were bought at a price. Therefore honour God with your body' (1 Corinthians 6:19—20). Only with this basis clearly understood can we go on to look at its practical outworking, which we shall do from two angles.

Firstly, it is an individual responsibility. The Bible puts it like this: 'Each one should use whatever gift he has received to serve others, faithfully administering God's grace in its various forms' (1 Peter 4:10). The precise point about stewardship is partially hidden by the fact that the NIV translators have taken unnecessary liberties with the Greek and rendered the plural noun *oikonomoi* by the phrase 'faithfully administering', but we can straighten things out as we go through the

text. The first thing to notice is that *every* Christian has
gifts for which he is responsible. The believer who opts
out of service in the world and responsibility in the
church, and who tries to shelter under the excuse that
he has nothing to offer is doing just that — sheltering
under an *excuse*. Peter says, 'Each . . . has received';
there are no exceptions. Beware of escaping the trap
of extravagant pride only to fall into the pit of false
humility. Let me quote some words from *The Song of
the Virgin* by Spiros Zodhiates: 'If you are leading a
useless life, you are not being humble, you are just
plain lazy . . . Many a man, while seriously believing
that he was exercising an acceptable humility, has
buried his talents in the earth, hidden his light under
a bushel, lived a useless life, when he might have been
a blessing to many . . . Our humility serves us falsely
when it leads us to shrink from any duty. The plea of
unfitness or inability is utterly insufficient to excuse
us . . . Your talent may be very small, so small that it
scarcely seems to matter whether you use it or not, so
far as its impression on the world or on other lives is
concerned. Yet no one can know what is small and what
is great in this life, in which every cause starts conse-
quences that reach into eternity.' Does that say anything to you? Does it challenge the level of your involvement in God's work? Does it point to laziness or com-
promise in a world crying out for help?

The second thing we see from Peter's statement is
that every gift is an expression of *'God's grace* in its
various forms'. No talent or gift is of our own making
or deserving; all are given to us freely by God's unmerited favour. Paul puts it like this: 'What do you have
that you did not receive? And if you did receive it, why
do you boast as though you did not?' (1 Corinthians
4:7.) The point is clear. Write down all the talents,
gifts and abilities you possess. Then rub out all those

you did not receive as a result of God's free, unmerited generosity. The entire list will remain!

The third thing to notice is that God's grace does come in 'various forms'. Not everybody has the same gifts, talents or abilities. Paul recognized this quite clearly: 'Are all apostles? Are all prophets? Are all teachers? Do all work miracles? Do all have gifts of healing? Do all speak in tongues? Do all interpret?' (1 Corinthians 12:29—30) The answer, by inference, is in the negative. Christians vary in their gifts as much as in their temperaments — but all have some gifts, and for the exercise of those gifts they are accountable to God. When the American statesman Daniel Webster was asked what was the most important subject that had ever occupied his attention, he replied, 'My personal responsibility.' All Christians should capture something of that spirit, remembering that 'each one of us will give an account of himself to God' (Romans 14:12). There is no room for envy, jealousy or covetousness with regard to anyone else's gifts. They are all given by God's grace, and should cause us to rejoice in them as greatly as we rejoice in our own. Our concern is to be with the use of God's gifts, not with their distribution!

Secondly, it is an irresistible responsibility. We cannot escape from it, or shake it off. No Christian has the right to say, 'I am honoured to be a son, delighted to be a saint and happy to be a soldier, but I would rather not be a steward.' He does not have that option. He cannot be excused from his responsibility to make use of the gifts God has given him.

Let me illustrate this from one simple command given by Jesus to his disciples. Just before his ascension into heaven, he told them of the coming of the Holy Spirit upon them, and added, 'And you will be my witnesses in Jerusalem, and in all Judea and Samaria, and to all the ends of the earth' (Acts 1:8). Notice that this was not an *option;* the disciples were not told that they *could* be Christ's witnesses, or that they *might* be. The statement was imperative — 'You *will* . . .' So today, every Christian has that same responsibility. He is a witness, he is a steward by the very fact that he is saved, and the only question open to debate is whether he is a good steward or a bad one.

But the matter does not end there, because the fact of the matter is that the world will judge the truth of Christianity by the credibility of the witnesses. I have always been deeply challenged by Jesus' statement: 'He who is not with me is against me, and he who does not gather with me scatters' (Matthew 12:30). It would surely be difficult to put our responsibility more strongly than that. If you are a Christian, then presumably you have no problem with the first part of that statement. You *are* with Christ. You are on his side, trusting him as your Saviour, acknowledging him to be your Lord. But what about the second part? Are you gathering with him or scattering? Is your life an influence in drawing people to Christ or in driving them from him? Are people more likely to believe the Christian gospel because of the way you live, or is your life more likely to make it more difficult for them to believe? Is your life a Bible or a libel? Privilege and responsibility are two sides of one coin. To be a steward is a great privilege, but it is also a great responsibility, one that is individual and irresistible.

2. The range of Christian stewardship

Let me illustrate a sense in which this section of our study is unnecessary. Soon after a young friend of mine became a Christian she was telling some other young people what a great difference Christ had made in her life. She spoke about her church life, her new understanding of the Bible, her change in attitude at home, and so on. After listening to her for some time, one of her friends asked, 'But what about the other parts of your life?' Nancy immediately replied, 'But there are no "other parts". Christ is the Lord of the whole of my life!' That was a fine answer, and underlines what we have already seen about stewardship. As Christians, we are stewards of all we are and all we have. There are no 'other parts'. Yet that statement can actually be so vague that we might be tempted to escape in generalities. To avoid this, let us look at just some of the things of which God holds us to be stewards.

Firstly, there is the stewardship of time. Writing to the Christians at Ephesus, Paul says, 'Be very careful, then, how you live — not as unwise but as wise, making the most of every opportunity, because the days are evil' (Ephesians 5:15—16). The Greek verb behind the phrase 'making the most of every opportunity' is *exagorazo,* which literally means 'to buy out'. It comes from the market-place and is the kind of word you might use about someone buying up an entire stock. This is the spirit Paul has in mind. He sees the Christian recognizing that time is a precious commodity which should be used to its fullest capacity.

In the late 1850s a ten-year-old boy called Thomas Edison tried to solve the problem of human flight by persuading another lad to take a vast overdose of salts! The experiment was a dismal and no doubt painful disaster. But by the time Edison was eighty years of age he had taken out over 1,000 patents. He won the Nobel Prize for Physics in 1915. He became known as 'the man whose workshop changed the world'. He invented the phonograph and the electric light bulb, and played a major part in the invention and development of the microphone, the telephone and many other scientific instruments. He worked about eighteen hours a day, slept only when he was tired and ate only when he was hungry. It was this remarkable man who once said, 'Time is not a commodity that can be stored for future use. It must be invested hour by hour or else it is gone for ever.' Edison's life-style may not be the wisest pattern to follow, but every Christian should see the point of his obvious logic and carry it into the stewardship of his time. While the world speaks about *spending* time, the Bible speaks about *buying* it! Are you sure you are on the right side of the counter?

Secondly, there is the stewardship of leisure. This is often overlooked when thinking of the stewardship of time, but it is vitally important. Somebody suggested to a friend of mine that a Christian should never take a complete rest on holiday, but should use it for some specific evangelistic activity, such as a beach mission, a youth camp, tract distribution or door-to-door visitation. He even suggested to my friend that his 'day off' each week should be invested in the same way. When my friend protested that surely there was a time when it was right to take a rest, the other man replied, 'Certainly not. Look at the devil. He never takes a rest.' 'And since when', my friend countered, 'should a Christian follow the devil's example?' Collapse of hyper-active Christian!

A wise old preacher once said, 'There is a time for everything, and a season for every activity under heaven' (Ecclesiastes 3:1) and without doubt there is a time for sensible, restorative rest, change and recreation. Jesus made this clear when he invited his disciples: 'Come with me by yourselves to a quiet place and get some rest' (Mark 6:31), and it is very important to notice that he said this at a time when 'many people were coming and going'. It was while they were surrounded by people in great physical and spiritual need that Jesus withdrew his disciples for a break in order to recharge their batteries.

The question of the use of leisure is difficult to get into perspective in today's world. With the pace of life getting faster all the time, people are finding it more and more difficult to use their leisure wisely, even though the amount becoming available is gradually increasing. Vance Havner tells the story of two people who discovered that their home towns were fairly near to each other. One of them said, 'You know, I used to visit your town once a week back in the horse and buggy days. It took me the whole day to get there and back, but I enjoyed it. I could do it in half an hour now by car, but I just don't have the time!' When you come to think of it, 'I don't have the time' is a strange phrase to use, because we all have exactly the same amount of time — twenty-four hours in every day. The all-important thing is how we use it.

Let me apply this to the question of leisure. The Christian should make a specific assessment of his leisure in terms of the total stewardship of his time — and be prepared to do some hard and careful thinking. To touch on an obvious area, I do not think that a Christian is investing his leisure time wisely if he spends hour after hour, night after night, lolling in front of a television set, using it as chewing gum for the eyes. There is something pathetically sad about the thought of countless people all over the country allowing a one-eyed god to dictate their entire thinking processes for 25% of their waking hours, bathing their minds in politics and pop, drama and detergents, overkill and underwear. It is calculated that by the time the average child is fourteen years old he will have seen 18,000 people violently assaulted or killed on television. By the time he leaves school he will have seen 350,000 commercials, and all in all will spend ten years of his life watching television! By any reckoning, that is a mite too much; in terms of a Christian's stewardship of time it is criminal. If a man's leisure-time exercise consists only of changing channels it is not only his legs which will become atrophied.

Of course, television is not wrong in itself. It is something that God has allowed man to discover and develop and is therefore capable of being used to enrich his life. Television can be a great educator, not only explicitly through the Open University and schools programmes but in the wider areas of current affairs, history, travel, nature and the like. It can also be a marvellous entertainer, in the fields of comedy, sport, music and so on. But for too many Christians it has become a deceptive dictator, robbing them of so much and giving them so little. As M.R.De Haan says, 'If you have half a mind to turn on television, it is all you will need for many programmes.' There is no doubt that many Christians would find their lives revolutionized if they adopted a wholly biblical approach to television, which is perhaps the major factor in the ordering of our leisure time.

Yet the whole question of leisure must be examined wisely in the context of our age, our work, our health and other relevant factors. To be absurd for a moment, it would be a little less than wise for a ninety-three-year old Christian who decided he was not getting enough exercise suddenly to join evening classes for all-in wrestling! Equally, a healthy teenager who spends all his working hours sitting at a desk is not wise to spend all his off-work times sunk in an armchair reading books. The balance, of course, lies between the two, but the principle remains the same. Examine your leisure time as part of your stewardship. Look upon it as something the Lord has given you to enrich your life. Plan it

sensibly — *and then enjoy it!* It need not interfere with
your sanctification!

Thirdly, there is the stewardship of money.   In the Old
Testament, we read of the building of the great temple
in Jerusalem about 1,000 B.C. King David gave overall
direction to his son Solomon, then charged the people
of Israel with the responsibility of raising the vast sum
of money needed. In an amazing demonstration of generosity and sacrifice a sum equalling many millions of
pounds was given — without a single jumble sale, lottery
or bingo session! In the Bible's words, they gave 'freely
and wholeheartedly to the Lord' (1 Chronicles 29:9).
David was naturally delighted at this tremendous response and gathered the people together to praise the
Lord. In the course of his prayer he said this: 'Now,
our God, we give you thanks, and praise your glorious
name. But who am I, and who are my people, that we
should be able to give as generously as this? Everything
comes from you, and *we have given you only what
comes from your hand.'*

Here is a fundamental principle which underlies the
whole question of the stewardship of money — and, indeed, of anything else. Even if we were to give everything we possessed, we would have given nothing that
was not in the first place God's gift to us. This immediately puts all our financial giving in its true biblical
perspective. Take the question of tithing, for instance.
Assuming for a moment that a Christian, on reading
Scripture, comes to the conclusion that he should give
at least one-tenth of his gross income directly to God's
service, this does not mean that the remaining nine-
tenths is his to do with as he pleases. The principle,
remember, is that *ten-tenths* of his money belongs to
the Lord, and that he is therefore as responsible to the
Lord for the use of the nine-tenths as for the one-tenth.

On that basis, should you be asking yourself some

serious questions about the amount you spend on
clothing, or records, or food, or sport, or entertainment,
or other things? You might even need to look again at
that matter of tithing. When you do, you might consider these words by Kenneth Prior: 'It could be argued
that in the Old Testament tithes were *paid,* and therefore do not, strictly speaking, come under the heading
of giving at all. Christian giving only begins when we
give more than a tenth.'

On the basis of all of this, let me ask you this question: are you giving to God what is right — *or what is
left?* Does God come first in your stewardship of
money? A friend of mine who has been in Christian service for many years once said, 'Unconsecrated Christian
giving is the greatest hindrance to Christian progress,'
and I am inclined to agree with him. It hinders progress
in the spiritual life of the Christian concerned, because
God has promised blessing to the giver; and it hinders
progress in Christian work, which so often has to limp
along because of lack of funds. Where do you stand in
this whole area? Are you part of the problem or part
of the answer?

Fourthly, *there is the stewardship of our special gifts.*
At the end of what we could call the parable of the
stewardship of life, Jesus establishes a vitally important
principle: 'From everyone who has been given much,
much will be demanded; and from the one who has been
entrusted with much, much more will be asked' (Luke
12:48). In a nutshell, this means that your responsibility
as a Christian steward exactly matches the gifts God has
given you.

A young man once became blind through illness. He
lived, however, to a ripe old age and just before he died
he prayed, 'I thank thee, Father, for the gift of blindness.' His name? Louis Braille, inventor of the most
widely-used blind reading system in the world. I find

that deeply challenging. If he could say that about blindness, what of the person with sight, health, strength and a host of other gifts? Some have the gift of friendship, some the gift of communication, some the gift of hospitality, some a great ability to organize, some have great practical ability, some the gift of administration, some the gift of music, some can type, others have the gift of writing. The list is endless — and so is the need for their deployment in the church today.

We need, however, to add a careful rider here. I can remember the time early in my Christian life when I felt that my 9—5 office job was merely a means of earning a living, and that life's *real* work came after office hours, when I was involved in the church, the youth fellowship, wider evangelistic work and other directly 'Christian' service. Looking back now, I can see that I was making a fundamental, if enthusiastic, error. The fact of the matter is that I ought to have seen my 'secular' work in the same light as my 'Christian' service — part of the total stewardship of life, and for which I was equally answerable to God in every way. The ability to work is God-given and to use that gift honourably and efficiently is part of the Christian's total stewardship.

However, what we particularly have in mind here is the use of 'secular' gifts in 'spiritual' settings, and in this area it is important to grasp this one great principle: whatever your particular gifts, God can use them for the extension of his kingdom, the building of his church, the blessing of his people, the conversion of sinners and the glory of his name. What an exhilarating thought! And what dimension it gives to the Bible's clear command: 'Do not neglect your gift'! (1 Timothy 4:14.)
Fifthly, there is the stewardship of the gospel. There is a sense in which this has already been covered by the

use of all of our gifts in the work of the kingdom of God, but perhaps one extra word is needed. Paul's assessment was this: 'So then, men ought to regard us as servants of Christ and as those entrusted with the secret things of God' (1 Corinthians 4:1); and what was true of Paul in a special way is true of every Christian in a general way. Not every Christian is called to be a preacher, lead a Bible class, serve as a missionary, or take a position of public leadership in the church, but every Christian is called upon to share in the evangelization of the world.

The gospel has been given to you as a sacred trust. Are you a good steward of what Paul calls 'the secret things of God'? If every other member of your church did as much as you to reach people with the gospel, would your church be building an extension or closing down? Someone once put it like this: 'To be "in Christ" is to be involved. You did not choose to be in the business of bringing men to Christ. You chose Christ and you are in the business. You may shrink from it, fumble it, refuse to do it, but you are never absolved from the fact and responsibility of it.' Are you a faithful steward of the gospel?

3. The reward of Christian stewardship

Although there are some real difficulties in interpreting the parable of the talents in Matthew 25, one principle stands out very clearly: God will grant eternal rewards to his people according to their stewardship. In the parable, the man who had been given five talents and the man who had been given two talents were both rewarded with their master's words: 'Well done, good and faithful servant! You have been faithful with a few things; I will put you in charge of many things' (Matthew

25:21, 23). Paul takes up the same point when he writes, 'For we must all appear before the judgement seat of Christ, that each one may receive what is due to him for the things done while in the body, whether good or bad' (2 Corinthians 5:10). There is no question here of a Christian being lost, for the judgement of which Paul is speaking is one of the Christian's *works* and not strictly of the Christian. No steward will be turned out of the household of God, but there will be differences in the rewards they will receive, and these will not be according to their fame but according to their faithfulness. That being so, surely every Christian should seek to be a wise and trustworthy steward of all that God has given him, living and longing for the day when he will hear his heavenly Master's 'Well done'.

A medical student once took a First Class Honours degree at Edinburgh University. His friends speculated about his future. Would he go on to earn further degrees, aim at a professorship, or capitalize in some other way on his ability and achievement? To their astonishment, he announced that he was going to the foreign mission-field. Stunned that he should apparently throw away such dazzling prospects, they told him, 'But that is no way to get on in the world.' His reply was simple and unanswerable: *'Which world?'*

To be a good steward in God's eyes is infinitely more important than to be a great success in the world's, and the rewards are beyond comparison.

7.

A V.I.P.
No ordinary person

7.

A V.I.P.
No ordinary person

There is no such person as an ordinary Christian. There are *average* Christians (too many of them) and *normal* Christians (too few of them), but none who can properly be described as ordinary. Let me try to explain.

It must surely be obvious that the average Christian's spiritual standard of living is a long way below the pattern we see in the New Testament. Vance Havner has said that we are so sub-normal that if we ever became normal people would think we were abnormal! His assessment is so true that the humour gets lost in the tragedy. The sad and simple fact is that there are far too many *average* Christians in our churches today. As for *normal* Christians, Watchman Nee discusses this at the beginning of his well-known book *The Normal Christian Life,* where he says that his aim is 'to show that it is something very different from the life of the average Christian'. He then goes on to say that the normal Christian life is one of godliness, victory, progress and spiritual health, a life filled with Christ. On that assessment it is surely not difficult to come to the conclusion that there are far too many average Christians and far too few who are normal.

Nevertheless, I maintain that there is no Christian who is ordinary, and I would take Ephesians 2 as a starting-point. It is a fascinating chapter, listing a catalogue of contrasts between what these Christians were before and after their conversion to Christ. The contrasts all hinge on two little phrases: 'at that time' (v. 12), and 'but now' (v. 13). Paul tells his readers that they *were* 'separate from Christ' (v. 12), but they *are now* 'in Christ Jesus' (v. 13); they *were* 'excluded from citizenship in Israel' but they *are now* 'fellow-citizens with God's people' (v. 19); they *were* 'foreigners to the covenants of the promise', but they *are now* 'members of God's household' (v. 19); they *were* 'far away' but *are now* 'brought near' (v. 13); they *were* 'dead in transgressions' but *are now* 'alive with Christ' (v. 5). What amazing and total contrasts! No wonder Paul is able to write elsewhere, 'Therefore, if anyone is in Christ, he is a new creation; the old has gone, the new has come!' (2 Corinthians 5:17.)

What a telling phrase that is! The Christian is not an improvement, he is an innovation. He is a new creation, a new and different person altogether, and it is in that sense that we can say that there is no such person as an ordinary Christian. Every Christian is extraordinary. He is not just 'one of the crowd'; he has been set apart from the crowd. He is in a minority in the world, what we could properly call a *select* minority, *and God has made the selection.*

Of the many places where this particular truth is emphasized, none is clearer than the following definition of God's people: 'But you are a chosen people, a royal priesthood, a holy nation, a people belonging to God, that you may declare the praises of him who called you out of darkness into his wonderful light' (1 Peter 2:9). Notice the adjectives: 'chosen', 'royal', 'holy', 'belonging to God'. Hardly ordinary, are they? Yet they apply to every Christian in the world without exception. Then why do they seem such extravagant definitions when applied to so many of today's professing Christians? I believe there are two reasons.

Firstly, there are many people masquerading as Christians with no genuine experience of Christ and therefore no right to that name. There is a story about a rich American couple on holiday in Florida. On the first day the husband got into difficulties while swimming and was dragged ashore by two lifeguards. One of them turned to the man's anxious wife and said, 'I think we should give him artificial respiration.' With a disdainful gasp, the wife snapped, 'How dare you give my husband anything artificial? We can afford the real thing!' The story is hardly memorable, but at least serves to point out that there is a difference between the artificial and the real — and there are too many people in our churches today without the real thing as far as Christian experience is concerned. They have never experienced the new birth and are therefore incapable of sustaining the new life. They are kept going by the artificial respiration of religious observance, theological beliefs or respectable behaviour — but they have no genuine spiritual life.

Secondly, many Christians have failed to grasp the reality of their spiritual position. They have never discovered at any depth what the Bible has to say about their status and significance as Christians. Sometimes over-anxious about the ways in which they differ from other Christians, sometimes nervously preoccupied with whether there is some other 'experience' they ought to have, they fail to realize the status and resources that are already theirs in common with all other Christians. Now there are obviously many ways in which Christians differ from one another, as do members of any other body of people. They are not all highly intelligent, or extrovert, or wealthy. They are not all left-handed, or lorry drivers or vegetarians. But there are things — tremendously significant things — that *are* true of every Christian in the world without exception and that mark the Christian out as a V.I.P. — a Very Important Person. Here are four of them, all found in that one verse in Peter's letter.

1. The Christian's dynasty

The first thing Peter says of Christians is that they are 'a chosen people'. When we hear a phrase like 'God's chosen race' or 'God's chosen people' our thoughts go straight to the people of Israel in the Old Testament, and, of course, that is where the phrase has its origins.

When Abraham (Abram at the time, but we will use his later name for convenience) was seventy-five years old, God called him to leave home for a journey into the unknown. He had probably never heard of the land of Canaan that God promised to him, but his mind was filled with an even greater promise, God's word to him that 'I will make you into a great nation' (Genesis 12:2). Although childless, Abraham's obedience to the command and his acceptance of the promise were immediate and total. The next chapters of Genesis tell a story of such drama, adventure and courage as to make the most racy modern thriller read like a nursery-rhyme by comparison. When he was a hundred years old, Abraham's wife Sarah gave birth to a son, Isaac, and at last the way seemed open for God's pledge to be fulfilled. Isaac would be the link between Abraham and the unborn generations to come who would form the 'great nation' God had promised.

But Abraham's greatest test was yet to come. Almost unbelievably, God directed him to take Isaac and put him to death as a sacrifice on Mount Moriah. In a staggering act of obedience, Abraham took Isaac up the mountain, made an altar, bound Isaac upon it, and was about to plunge his knife into Isaac's body when God

dramatically intervened and substituted a sacrificial
animal which he had prepared. Abraham's faith had
been proved in an amazing way, and God's promise was
immediately renewed: 'I swear by myself, declares the
Lord, that because you have done this and have not
withheld your son, your only son, I will surely bless you
and make your descendants as numerous as the stars
in the sky and as the sand on the seashore' (Genesis
22:16—17).

The story then widens and deepens in the most
amazing way. Isaac's twin son Jacob (whose name was
later changed to Israel) had twelve sons, who eventually
gave their names to the twelve tribes of the new nation.
The new people's history then took an erratic and unstable course until they were swept off to captivity in
Egypt for four hundred years. Then came the remarkable story of the exodus under Moses, the forty years
of wandering in the wilderness and eventually the
settlement in the promised land of Canaan. Of course,
that is the merest skeleton of the story, but through it
all runs one central theme: God chose out a people for
himself and guided and guarded their ways until his
purposes for them were fulfilled. Without this underlying theme, the Old Testament is no more than a scrap-
book of unconnected incidents; with it, the whole
drama can be seen as one story, the story of God's
dealings with his people.

Turning to the New Testament, we discover a phrase
which links all of this with Peter's description of Christians as being a chosen people. It is where Paul tells the
Galatians that although he is a full-blooded Jew he has
nothing in which he can boast spiritually 'except in the
cross of our Lord Jesus Christ, through which the world
has been crucified to me, and I to the world' (Galatians
6:14) and then goes on, 'Neither circumcision nor un-
circumcision means anything, what counts is a new

creation' (Galatians 6:15). What Paul is saying here is that the rituals and ceremonies of the Old Testament are unable to make a person a Christian; he needs to be born again, to become a 'new creation'. Then comes the phrase we are looking for, for Paul immediately adds, 'Peace and mercy to all who follow this rule, even to *the Israel of God'* (Galatians 6:16).

Here is the link between the drama of the Old Testament and the life of a twentieth-century Christian. Every Christian in the world today, whether Jew or Gentile by origin, is a member of the new, spiritual Israel — what Paul calls 'the Israel of God' — and as such part of the 'chosen people' of which Peter speaks. Have you grasped this? And have you thought it through to an understanding of some of the implications that flow from it? Here are two of them.

Firstly, we are involved in the purposes of God. In an itinerant ministry I have the privilege of travelling to many famous places that I would not otherwise visit. To stand at Bannockburn in Scotland, or on the Mayflower Steps in Plymouth, or under the shadow of the Berlin Wall, or at the Parthenon in Athens, or on the Golden Horn in Istanbul, or at the spot in Dallas where John F. Kennedy was assassinated, always fills me with a sense of history, a tingling sensation that my own little life is something more than an isolated incident. But there is an even greater way in which we can experience a sense of history. Oliver Cromwell once said, 'What is history but God's unfolding of himself?' Someone else put it even more succinctly by saying that 'History is *his* story.' It is the record of God at work, in the unknown reaches of the universe, in the world around us, on the whole, vast human stage. John Stott has a superb comment on this in his book *The Message of Galatians.* He writes, 'There is a great need in the church today for a biblical, Christian philosophy of

history. Most of us are short-sighted and narrow-minded.
We are so preoccupied with current affairs in the twentieth century that neither the past nor the future has
any great interest for us. We cannot see the wood for the
trees. We need to step back and try to take in the whole
counsel of God, his everlasting purpose to redeem a
people for himself through Jesus Christ. Our philosophy
of history must make room not only for the centuries
after Christ, but for the centuries before him, not only
for Abraham and Moses but for Adam, through whom
sin and judgement entered the world, and for Christ,
through whom salvation has come. If we include the beginning of history, we must include its consummation
also, when Christ returns in power and great glory, to
take his power and reign. The God revealed in the Bible
is working to a plan. He 'accomplishes all things according to the counsel of his will' (Ephesians 1:11).

The Christian who knows his Bible can therefore rejoice that in a very special way he is caught up in the
purposes of God. His birth, life, conversion and circumstances are not accidents, nor the result of blind fate —
they are part of history and therefore part of 'his story'.
They are prepared, planned and purposeful. Bertrand
Russell, the famous philosopher, once wrote, 'You are
an eddying speck of dust; a harassed, driven leaf', but
the Christian knows better. He sees that he is part of
God's eternal and unchanging purpose. As Matthew
Henry put it, 'All true Christians are a chosen generation;
they make one family, a sort of species of people distinct from the common world.'

This is the first thing that follows from the fact that
Christians are described as 'a chosen people'. At an individual level, it means that if you are a Christian you are
linked to every other Christian in history and are
brought with them into the orbit of Paul's great conviction that 'in all things God works for the good of those

who love him, who have been called according to his purpose' (Romans 8:28). What a philosophy of life to have in today's neurotic world!

Secondly, we inherit the promises of God. While Mary was expecting the baby Jesus she visited her near relation Elizabeth, who was later to become the mother of John the Baptist. In an extraordinary prophecy inspired by the Holy Spirit, Elizabeth told Mary that she was to be 'the mother of my Lord' (Luke 1:43). No doubt remembering an earlier promise made to her by an angel, Mary responded with a marvellous song of praise to God which ends, 'He has helped his servant Israel, remembering to be merciful to Abraham and his descendants for ever, even as he said to our fathers' (Luke 1:54—55). Now the important thing to notice is that the promise made to Abraham was linked with the birth of Jesus and the salvation of believers. Immediately after the birth of John the Baptist, his father Zacharias, filled with the Holy Spirit, poured out his praise to God for the coming of Jesus into the world as Saviour, Redeemer and Lord, and said that in doing so God was acting 'to show mercy to our fathers and to remember his holy covenant, the oath he swore to our father Abraham' (Luke 1:72—73). Again, the promise to Abraham, the coming of Jesus and the salvation of God's people, 'the Israel of God', are all linked together.

An Arab once told me of the importance of Abraham in Muslim traditions. There are apparently nearly 200 references to him in the Koran, the sacred book of Islam, and as a great prophet and leader he is commonly referred to as the father of the faithful. But the Bible's teaching goes much further than that and says that the true children of Abraham are those who trust in Abraham's God for their salvation; *and that as such they share the promises of God.* Just as surely as he has proved the promise of salvation to be true, so he can prove the truth of all the other promises that God makes to believers in his Word. In C.H. Spurgeon's *The Cheque-book of the Bank of Faith,* a book of daily Bible readings, he compares each of the Bible's promises to a cheque drawn in the Christian's favour and signed by God. All the Christian has to do is to take it, endorse it with his own name, and 'come to heaven's bank in order to receive the promised amount'. To some people, that sounds too simple to be true, but I am convinced that this matter of active faith in the declared promises of God is a vital key to healthy, progressive Christian living.

Preaching once in a church in Spokane, Washington, I saw these words written on the wall: 'You can never starve a man who is feeding on the promises of God.' That is a change of metaphor from the one used by Spurgeon, but it is not a change of truth. If you are a Christian, you are a child of God, a member of his family, one of the 'chosen people', and as such the promises of God are yours. Find them, know them, claim them and live in their proved experience. It is part of your heritage to do so.

2. The Christian's dignity

Of the four phrases Peter uses in this verse, three are taken from Exodus 19:5—6, words spoken by God through Moses to the people of Israel at Mount Sinai. One of the titles given to them there was 'a kingdom of priests' (Exodus 19:6) and what makes this such a striking phrase is that throughout the Old Testament kings and priests held separate offices. There is at least one vivid illustration of the importance of this. King Uzziah was an outstanding leader who achieved unusual success as a military general and civil administrator. But we are told that 'After Uzziah became powerful, his pride led to his downfall' (2 Chronicles 26:16). The real crunch came when he went into the temple one day to burn incense on the altar, a function strictly reserved for the priesthood. Azariah the high priest rushed in with eighty of his assistants and told Uzziah that he had usurped his authority, warning him to 'leave the sanctuary, for you have been unfaithful; and you will not be honoured by the Lord God' (2 Chronicles 26:18). Caught in the very act of defying God's clear command, Uzziah was furiously unrepentant, but even as the anger broke out in his heart so, to the astonishment of everybody present, leprosy broke out on his forehead. He was immediately bundled out of the temple, relieved of his office, and excluded from the temple for the rest of his life.

Nothing could demonstrate more vividly the clear distinction between the offices of king and priest under the Old Testament dispensation; yet in the passage we are studying Peter unites both in describing Christians as 'a royal priesthood'. John does the same when he ascribes praise 'to him who loves us and has freed us from our sins by his blood, and has made us to be *a kingdom and priests* to serve his God and Father' (Revelation 1:5–6). Again, John tells us of those before the throne of God who sing praises to the One who has redeemed men to God and has 'made them to be *a kingdom and priests* to serve our God' (Revelation 5:10). To go back to Peter's phrase, Christians form 'a royal priesthood'. Spiritually speaking, they have the dual dignity of being both kings and priests. But what does this mean in terms of practical, everyday living?

Firstly, as a king you can exhibit God's power. Of all the terms used in these studies, 'a king' surely seems the most difficult to accept and to demonstrate in everyday terms. Is this a bit of enthusiastic exaggeration, perhaps? A slight case of religious licence? Not a bit of it! In his commentary on Revelation, Luther Poellot says that the kingdom to which Christians belong 'is Christ's kingdom of grace and glory. Its members have royal power and dignity. By faith they possess all that Christ, their one great King, has. They rule with him. They concur in all that he does. They do with him all that he does. They own the universe, the world, and all things in the world.'

But let me try to be a little more practical. A Christian reigns in a situation by overcoming it, by subduing it, by mastering it, by coming through it with his character strengthened, by using it to demonstrate the grace, love, power and mercy of God. The Christian reigns by overcoming the world, crucifying the flesh and successfully resisting the devil. In fine, the Christian is seen to reign as he demonstrates the all-sufficient power of God at work in his life.

Secondly, as a priest you can enter God's presence. Under the Old Covenant, no ordinary Jew was allowed to go beyond the Court of the Israelites in the temple. Only the high priest could go into the inner sanctuary, the Most Holy Place. In New Testament days that inner sanctuary was barred by a huge curtain, but at the moment of Christ's death there was a violent earthquake and 'the curtain of the temple was torn in two from top to bottom' (Matthew 27:51). It must have been a frightening moment for anyone who saw it happen, but it symbolizes a glorious truth for the Christian. The writer to the Hebrews puts it like this: 'Therefore, brothers, since we have confidence to enter the Most Holy Place by the blood of Jesus, by a new and living way opened for us through the curtain, that is, his body, and since we have a great priest over the house of God, let us draw near to God with a sincere heart in full assurance of faith, having our hearts sprinkled to cleanse us from a guilty conscience and having our bodies washed with pure water' (Hebrews 10:19–22). Just as surely as the curtain was torn away from the Most Holy Place on that historic day, so for the Christian the spiritual barrier that kept him from God has been torn away by the death of Christ. What is more, every Christian is ordained as a priest and is officially authorized to enter God's presence at any time, on any matter, in all circumstances.

When Access credit cards were launched in Britain the compelling slogan used was 'Access takes the waiting out of wanting'. The message was clear: whatever you wanted you could get immediately by using that little plastic card. But the Christian has an even better 'Access card'. Paul tells us about it when he says of Jewish and Gentile Christians alike, 'Through [Christ] we both have access to the Father by one Spirit' (Ephesians 2:18). This 'card' may not always take the waiting out of wanting (in fact, it may at times take the wanting out of waiting!) but it does something much greater. It enables even the weakest Christian to bring all his needs, problems, fears, anxieties, sorrows and circumstances to God's throne of grace, knowing that there are sufficient resources there to meet his every need 'according to [God's] glorious riches in Christ Jesus' (Philippians 4: 19). And those riches are not affected by a change of government, a credit squeeze, a pay pause, a mini-budget, a rise in bank rate or a fall in share prices! As a priest, then, you have constant, immediate access to God by the prayer of faith. Let nothing rob you of this great privilege!

3. The Christian's duty

Peter now adds a third description of Christian people, and calls them 'a holy nation', and we shall come right to the practical heart of what this implies if we think in terms of the duty that being part of such a nation imposes on its members.

Firstly, it is a covenant duty.   The expression 'a holy nation' is one of the three phrases taken from Exodus 19, where God's words were given in the context of the covenant he established with Israel. Under that covenant, God promised to pour out great blessings on his people, but as we know from the story that unfolds after that, Israel forfeited many of these through disobedience. The lesson is surely clear. As we have seen, God's promises remain utterly trustworthy, but many are conditional on the Christian's obedience. The Christian is under the moral obligations of God's law. He is free from the law as a system of justification, but not as a yardstick of sanctification. *He is not forced to obey it in order to be saved; he is free to obey it because he is saved.* A new covenant assumes new conduct. In Paul's words, 'For God did not call us to be impure, but to live a holy life' (1 Thessalonians 4:7). That being so, too many Christians could be said to have missed their vocation. Not all Christians are called to be pastors, or evangelists, or similar public figures, but they are all called to live holy lives, lives that are morally superior to those of their unconverted contemporaries.

The link between the Christian's covenant and call is seen again in Peter's next phrase: '. . . that you may declare the praises of him who called you out of darkness into his wonderful light. Once you were not a people, but now you are the people of God; once you had not received mercy, but now you have received mercy.' In these phrases both what God has done for the Christian and what the Christian should do for God are intertwined. As Alan Stibbs remarks, 'So it is the company of erstwhile outsiders with no status and deserving judgement as sinners who, because of God's mercy,

towards them in Christ, and because they have come
to him, are told that they now constitute a community
characterized by election, royalty, priesthood, holiness
and privileged relation to God as his special people.
They are also told that what has thus happened to them,
and what they now are by God's doings, is intended to
proclaim or advertise to the universe the worthiness
of God's works and ways.' That puts it precisely!

Secondly, it is a constant duty.   This point is so obvious that it hardly needs more than the briefest comment. Just as we are not saved one day and lost the next,
a member of God's holy nation one day but disenfran-
chised the next, so our duty as members of that nation
remains constant and unchanged. The Christian should
never observe any particular day as 'holy' in *moral* terms,
for the simple reason that his duty to live a godly life is
constant. To call Sunday 'the Lord's Day' does not
imply that the other six belong to someone else! Just as
there is never a day when the Christian is not secure in
his salvation, so there should never be a day when he is
not diligent in his striving for sanctification. He is part
of a nation meant to be characterized by a distinctive
quality of life, and whose members should constantly
seek to live 'holy and godly lives' (2 Peter 3:11).

4. The Christian's destiny

A dictionary definition of 'destiny' is 'the purpose or
end to which any person or thing is destined or appointed' and that is a good definition to hold in mind as
we turn to take another look at Peter's description of
Christians as 'a people belonging to God'. Here are two
strands of truth woven into this particular title.

Firstly, there is a selection we cannot fathom.   In an
earlier study we came across Paul's statement that we
were 'by nature objects of wrath' (Ephesians 2:3). The

Amplified Bible renders that particular phrase, 'children of God's wrath and heirs of his indignation'. Now hold that terrible description alongside the same version's rendering of Peter's phrase here, which is 'God's own special purchased people'. What a staggering thing! Born under the righteous wrath and judgement of God, you have become one of his own special, purchased people, on whom he has promised to lavish his love for all eternity. Can you understand that? Can you fathom it out?

Johanna-Ruth Dobschiner was a fifteen-year old Jewess when Hitler invaded Holland in 1940. By 1944 her parents and two brothers had been snatched away by the Nazis in their anti-Semitic purge. Johanna-Ruth went underground and, by one means or another, continued to escape the fate of thousands of her fellow Jews. She also came to know the Lord Jesus Christ as her own personal Saviour, and eventually told her story in a book entitled *Selected to Live*. The primary reference in the title is to her miraculous survival of the Nazi war machine, but it is also a perfect description of her spiritual salvation — and of that of every Christian. A Christian has been selected to live; to live essentially in Christ, to live effectively for Christ, and to live eternally with Christ. And it is a selection we cannot fathom.

Secondly, there is a security which cannot fail.   In calling Christians 'a people belonging to God' Peter is speaking not about a passing phase of experience, but a destiny; and for the Christian that means the certainty of spending eternity in heaven. The journey may be long or short, the road rough or smooth, our health good or bad, our work large or small — but our destiny is certain and assured.

Nobody made this clearer than Jesus himself when he told his followers, 'In my Father's house are many· rooms; if it were not so, I would have told you. I am going there to prepare a place for you. And if I go and prepare a place for you, I will come back and take you to be with me that you also may be where I am' (John 14:2—3). God has selected us, not merely to engage in his earthly programme, but to enjoy his eternal presence, and every Christian should seek to live in the conscious certainty that each day takes him nearer to that glorious experience.

It has been said that a man's life is influenced more by his expectations than by his experiences. If that is so, what a vast difference there should be between the life of the Christian and that of the unbeliever! What are your expectations? And how do they affect your life? Here are two quotations, each from a person whose writings have been read by millions, and each speaking about his own personal expectations for the future.

'There is darkness without and when I die there will be darkness within. There is no splendour, no vastness anywhere; only triviality for a moment, and then nothing.'

'For I am convinced that neither death nor life, neither angels nor demons, neither the present nor the future, nor any powers, neither height nor depth, nor anything else in all creation, will be able to separate us from the love of God that is in Christ Jesus our Lord' (Romans 8:38—39).

The first statement was made by Bertrand Russell. He was a peer of the realm, a philosopher, a scientist, a mathematician, a political theorist and a Nobel Prize winner.

The second statement was made by the apostle Paul — a real V.I.P.!

8.

A Christian
The noble nickname

8.

A Christian
The noble nickname

It came as a great surprise to me when I first discovered how seldom the Bible mentions the word 'Christian'. Today, we use it more than any other to describe a follower of Christ, and in addition we speak about 'the Christian church', 'the Christian faith', 'the Christian way of life', and so on. Yet the word 'Christian' only occurs three times in the whole Bible.

Surprise number two came after I had looked closely at the three places where it occurs. Although the word 'Christian' was probably in fairly common use both inside and outside the church by the middle of the first century, it is likely that in not one of the three places in which we find it in the Bible was it used by Christians themselves.

The first reference is where we read that 'The disciples were first called Christians at Antioch' (Acts 11:26). This almost certainly means that they were called 'Christians' by other people, as a nickname or an easy means of identification. The second use of the word is by the heathen King Agrippa who snorted at the apostle Paul, 'Do you think that in such a short time you can persuade me to be a Christian?' (Acts 26:28.) The third occasion is where Peter writes to his fellow believers and says, 'However, if you suffer as a Christian, do not be ashamed, but praise God that you bear that name' (1 Peter 4:16). The point Peter seems to be making is that these believers were being linked with a Galilean trouble-maker called Jesus, who claimed to be 'the Christ', yet could not even offer a defence at his trial on a charge of blasphemy and was eventually executed by Pontius Pilate with the overwhelming popular consent of the Jewish people. To get tied up with a man like that was to risk all kinds of trouble, and to be a 'Christ'-ian was hardly anything to guarantee popularity.

These suggestions about the likely derivation of the word seem to be confirmed by the fact that about A.D. 116 the Roman historian Tacitus wrote about the persecution by the Emperor Nero of those 'whom the populous, or common people, were calling Christians'. The word 'Christian' was clearly a nickname, a term of abuse, associating people with an allegedly deluded Galilean preacher. Then something beautiful happened. The followers of Jesus took this derogatory nickname and began to use it among themselves. Eventually, it became a standard word of identification. They took the mud slung at them by their enemies and fashioned it into a badge of honour. Today, there is no better name that can be found for those who trust Christ as their Saviour, acknowledge Christ as their Lord and serve Christ as their King. *A Christian is a Christian!* As we take a closer look at the places where the word is used in the New Testament three important truths will emerge, helping us to consolidate the answer to our question: 'What in the world is a Christian?'

✝ A man under instruction

This is the essential truth underlying the first use of the word 'Christian' in the New Testament: 'The disciples were first called Christians at Antioch' (Acts 11:26), and the point seems clear and obvious on the surface of the text. Those called 'Christians' by unbelievers were called 'disciples' by the believers. The two titles were synonymous, or rather, they referred to the same people. That is important! I remember as a young Christian being harangued from the pulpit along these lines: 'You may be a Christian, but are you a disciple? You may have begun the Christian life, but have you moved on to that higher stage?' It all sounded very challenging, and therefore healthy and beneficial. But I have long since come to the conclusion that it is nothing of the sort.

We need to beware of enthusiasm that is not controlled by Scripture. Zeal alone is not necessarily a good thing. Paul's heart was breaking for his fellow Jews, of whom he wrote, 'For I can testify about them that they are zealous for God, but their zeal is not based on knowledge' (Romans 10:2). The thought of an express train roaring along at 100 m.p.h. sounds like exciting fun — but not if it has left the rails and is plunging down an embankment. Challenging people to a higher plane of Christian living is fine, necessary and important, but not if the way being taught has no basis in Scripture; and the Bible knows nothing of a two-tier system of Christianity in which there is a normative post-conversion leap on to a higher platform. Likewise, the Bible nowhere makes a distinction between a disciple and a Christian. What we do find (as the statement here in Acts 11 makes clear) is that the two words describe the same people. All the true disciples were Christians; all the true Christians were disciples.

This means that another way of asking, 'What in the world is a Christian?' is to ask, 'What in the world is a disciple?' and the answer to that question becomes pretty straightforward, because the word 'disciple' simply means 'a learner'. The disciple is a pupil, *a man*

under instruction. Now when people speak about 'the
disciples', they usually mean either the twelve men
specially selected by Jesus at the beginning of his public
ministry, or the seventy or so he commissioned later
on, or those who were gathered together on the Day of
Pentecost. But the Bible uses the word in a much wider
context. We read, for instance, of those who claimed,
'We are disciples of Moses!' (John 9:28), and of those
who were 'John's disciples' (Matthew 9:14). Later,
we are told that 'The Pharisees . . . sent their disciples
to [Jesus]' (Matthew 22:15–16). In both the Greek
and Jewish worlds philosophers and teachers gathered
to themselves groups of trainees, who sought to
understand and follow their line of teaching. The
common word for these people was 'disciples', so the
word was a natural one to use about the people who
attached themselves to Jesus and sought to assimilate
his teaching. With that background, we can now develop
the idea a little further, because when we examine what
the Bible has to say about the disciples of Jesus, we find
two particular characteristics demanded of them.

Firstly, a determined acquisition of the truth. On one
of my many visits to Macedonia I was taken to visit
a Christian recovering from a serious operation in a
hospital in Katerini. As we approached the ward I was
told that the man concerned was an elder in a church
in Berea: Immediately, my mind flew to the passage in
which we are told that the Jews at Berea 'were of more
noble character than the Thessalonians, for they received the message with great eagerness and examined
the Scriptures every day to see if what Paul said was
true' (Acts 17:11). I had hardly finished locating the
biblical reference when we rounded the corner and
stepped into the ward, and there was the man from
Berea, propped up in bed, reading his Bible! The
New Testament had come to life! Here was a worthy

successor to those noble Bereans, with a hunger for God's Word.

The first mark of a genuine disciple is that he is determined to acquire the truth — and not merely thoughts about the truth. We are living at a time when that will bear repeating. Although we are being deluged with new Bible translations and paraphrases, I am not convinced that today's rising generation of Christians know their Bibles any better. There is a world of difference between being able to express general ideas of what we might call Christian philosophy and actually knowing *what God's Word says*. Whan I was a young Christian it was considered important to memorize Scripture; that seems to be going out of fashion today, and I am sure that people are losing out as a result. David was able to say, 'I have hidden your Word in my heart that I might not sin against you' (Psalm 119:11). Can you say that? Are you hiding God's Word in your heart, consistently, regularly, diligently, seriously? Are you determined to acquire the truth of Scripture, or are you settling for vague religious slogans?

Of course, I am not suggesting that knowledge of Scripture comes easily. Salvation is by faith, but the knowledge of the Bible is by works! Jim Elliot, who was martyred by the Auca Indians in Ecuador in 1956 once wrote in his diary, 'I find I must drive myself to study, following the "ought" of conscience to gain anything at all from the Scripture, lacking any desire at times. It is important to learn respect and obedience to the "inner must" if godliness is to be a state of soul with me. I may no longer rely on pleasant impulses to bring me before the Lord. I must rather respond to principles I know to be right, whether I feel them to be enjoyable or not.' *I would suggest that you go back and read that extract again* because it contains a vital key to spiritual progress. The disciple must learn to obey what Jim

Elliot called the 'inner *must*' in order to acquire the truth of the Word of God.

Secondly, a diligent application of the truth. This takes the issue a vital stage further, and the crucial biblical principle on the subject is stated by Jesus when speaking to the Jews who had apparently believed on him: 'If you hold to my teaching, you are really my disciples' (John 8:31). The Amplified Bible fills out the meaning like this: 'If you abide in my word — hold fast to my teachings and live in accordance with them — you are truly my disciples.' It is not open to a true disciple to pick and choose what he hears, or the teachings with which he will agree, or by which he will live. A disciple is not like a scholar facing an examination and needing to attempt only five questions out of ten. Biblically, a disciple of Christ is expected to acquire all that he can and to apply everything that he acquires.

Jesus pressed this point home in a number of ways. For instance, he once said, 'My sheep listen to my voice; I know them, and they follow me' (John 10:27). Here is the dual response of hearing and obeying. As Al Martin has put it, 'The sheep had an open ear and an obedient foot,' and what was true of the sheep should be true of the scholar, the disciple. Then Jesus spoke of Christians being like branches of a vine, adding, 'This is to my Father's glory, that you bear much fruit, showing yourselves to be my disciples' (John 15:8). Again, the picture is clear. The branch is expected to bear the same fruit as the parent tree — and the Christian is expected to live out what he draws in. Then again, speaking to his disciples in the upper room in Jerusalem, Jesus said, 'A new commandment I give you: Love one another. As I have loved you, so you must love one another. All men will know that you are my disciples if you love one another' (John 13:34–35). The same truth comes through loud and clear: only by a diligent application of the truth does a man prove his Christian discipleship. Knowing the truth is not enough; there must be doing as well.

Following Britain's entry into the European Common Market, a British civil servant was discussing with a friend the difficulties of learning a new language. 'Oh, I'm all right,' his colleague replied, 'my French is excellent,' adding rather apologetically, 'except for the verbs'! Too many Christians are rather like that — fine on the nouns, feeble on the verbs. Grammatically speaking, a sentence is incomplete without a verb. Spiritually speaking, a man's profession to be a Christian is invalid unless it has verbs to back it up. The genuine disciple, the true Christian, is recognized not merely as someone who acquires truth, but as someone who applies it diligently in his life, proving his faith by his actions. As James has it, 'Do not merely listen to the word, and so deceive yourselves. *Do what it says*' (James 1:22). A Christian is a disciple, a man under instruction, and the true disciple will be marked by a determined acquisition of the truth and a diligent application of the truth.

2. A man under impulsion

The second use of the word 'Christian' in the New Testament is where King Agrippa says to Paul, 'Do you think that in such a short time you can persuade me to be a Christian?' (Acts 26:28.) The confrontation between Agrippa and Paul was rather like the one between Goliath and David. Herod Agrippa the Second was the great-grandson of Herod the Great and a special favourite of the Roman Emperor Nero. Anxious to ingratiate himself with his overlord, he had changed the name of Caesarea Philippi to Neronias in the emperor's honour. At the time concerned he was on a state visit with his queen Bernice (who was also his sister) to Porcius Festus, Procurator of Judea. Festus was holding the apostle Paul on three charges: treason, being the ringleader of an unauthorized rebel organization called the Nazarenes, and defiling the temple. The case had dragged on for about two years and had now reached a crucial point, because Paul had suddenly upset the apple-cart by exercising his right as a Roman citizen and demanding to be tried in Rome before the Emperor Nero himself.

This presented Festus with a tricky problem, because while he would want to file a report that would infer his wide knowledge of the case, he was in fact woefully ignorant about the ramifications of Jewish religious law. Suddenly, he saw a ray of hope! Agrippa was an expert in Jewish religious affairs; for twenty years he had had the prerogative of appointing the Jewish high priest in Jerusalem. What is more, he had expressed a wish to see and hear Paul for himself. By arranging a meeting between Agrippa and Paul, the wily Festus could neatly kill two bothersome birds with one stone.

With great pomp and ceremony, Agrippa and Bernice took their places in the audience hall, alongside the army's top brass and all the civic superstars. The whole glittering assembly settled into place.

Enter Paul! Although we have no further details of the scene, it is not difficult to picture Paul, weary and gaunt after two years in prison. Many deduce from certain phrases in his writings that he suffered from faulty or failing eyesight. Similarly, it is thought that he was not particularly handsome in his general appearance. Some people find evidence that he had an unimpressive voice and a rather poor manner of delivery. But as soon as Agrippa says, 'You have permission to speak for

yourself' (Acts 26:1), the whole balance of power changes
dramatically. Paul is suddenly clothed with divine
authority and holy boldness. With devastating clarity
he presents his case, marshalling his facts like a brilliant
lawyer. Even a bad-tempered interruption by Festus
fails to divert him, and at the end of the day even
Agrippa has to admit to Festus, 'This man could have
been set free, if he had not appealed to Caesar' (Acts
26:32).

It is a fascinating incident, but much more than that.
It is not only a narrative that lets us hear Paul's words,
it is an X-ray that enables us to see into his heart, and
what we find there is an overriding concern not merely
to prove the merits of his case, but to proclaim the
message of his Saviour. Pointedly reminding him that
the facts of the gospel were plain for all to see, and were
a fulfilment of Old Testament prophecy, he puts Agrippa
firmly on the spot with the daring question: 'King
Agrippa, do you believe the prophets? I know you do'
(Acts 26:27). The king's testy reply forms the trigger
for our present study: 'Do you think that in such a
short time you can persuade me to be a Christian?'
(Acts 26:28); and Paul's reply gives it its impetus:
'Short time or long — I pray God that not only you but
all who are listening to me today may become what
I am, except for these chains' (Acts 26:29).

Here was *a man under impulsion* — the impulsion of
the gospel. Paul was no pussyfooting apologist. He did
not content himself with superficial consent to a vague
theological concept. He had met with Christ, and from
then on he was a man under impulsion. When writing
of this to the church at Corinth he said, 'For Christ's
love compels us' (2 Corinthians 5:14). Christ's amazing
love in dying for sinners on the cross was the inex-
tinguishable fuel that fed the flames of Paul's mag-
nificent obsession. It was this which demanded his

soul, his life, his all. As Alan Redpath puts it in his
book *Blessings out of Buffetings,* 'Paul had looked with
Spirit-enlightened eyes into the heart of God, and
Christ's love for him gripped him, propelled him, im-
pelled him along one line of life to the exclusion of any
other attraction.' Let me underline this in two ways.

Firstly, he had an impulsion to give out.   Many Christians today have been described as being like the Cana-
dian rivers in winter — frozen at the mouth! Exactly the
opposite was true of Paul and the other apostles. When
the news of the resurrection of Jesus shook Jerusalem,
the local authorities became very agitated about the
apostles' preaching, and ordered them 'not to speak or
teach at all in the name of Jesus' (Acts 4:18). The reply
Peter and John gave could not have been clearer:
'Judge for yourselves whether it is right in God's sight
to obey you rather than God. For we cannot help speaking about what we have seen and heard' (Acts 4:20).
Inevitably, they were soon in trouble again, and on the
same charge. 'We gave you strict orders not to teach in
this name. Yet you have filled Jerusalem with your
teaching and are determined to make us guilty of this
man's blood' (Acts 5:28). The apostles' reply was firm
and final: 'We must obey God rather than men!' (Acts
5:29.)

That, for them, was the crucial issue. There was no
way round it. They were under divine orders to preach
and no human authority could change that. No wonder
we read that at the end of the session, 'The apostles
left the Sanhedrin, rejoicing because they had been
counted worthy of suffering disgrace for the Name.
Day after day, in the temple courts and from house to
house, they never stopped teaching and proclaiming
the good news that Jesus is the Christ' (Acts 5:41—42).

That same impulsion gripped Paul. His own testimony
could not have been clearer: 'Yet when I preach the

gospel I cannot boast, for I am compelled to preach. Woe
to me if I do not preach the gospel!' (1 Corinthians 9:16.)
So even when faced with the combined pomp and power
of Festus and Agrippa, Paul cannot hold back. He has to
speak the truth, not out of human enthusiasm for a religious cause, but as what a friend of mine used to call 'the
natural outcome of a spiritual income'. To go back to an
earlier metaphor, Paul did not have the impediment of
an icy mouth, but the impulsion of a heart on fire. He
was swept along by what Thomas Chalmers called 'the
expulsive power of a new affection'. He *had* to tell of
the One who had conquered him by love. Do you share
anything of that divine compulsion? Is sharing the
gospel with others merely a duty or even a drudgery?
Are you motivated by a church programme or an evangelistic scheme, or by an overwhelming sense of the love
of Christ in dying for you and for others on the cross of
Calvary? The answers reveal a great deal about you!

Secondly, he had an impulsion to get through.   Leighton
Ford has written a book on the priority of evangelism,
under the title *The Christian Persuader*. That is a fine
title because it comes straight from the pages of the
Bible. In the same passage from which we quoted
earlier, Paul says that the nub of the Christian's ministry
was this: 'We try to persuade men' (2 Corinthians 5:11).
What he is saying is that this is our business, our com-
mission, our concern, our aim. For Paul, it was not sufficient to get things said; he was not satisfied until the
things said were heard, understood and obeyed. He saw
his ministry in exactly those terms: 'Through [Christ]
and for his name's sake, we received grace and apostle-
ship to call people from among all the Gentiles *to the*
obedience that comes from faith' (Romans 1:5). Paul's
attitude was not 'There is the message; take it or leave
it.' *He had to get through,* and he was willing to do
anything in the will of God that would help him to

imprint the relevance of his message on the hearts of his hearers. He even dares to say this to unconverted Jews: 'For I could wish that I myself were cursed and cut off from Christ for the sake of my brothers, those of my own race, the people of Israel' (Romans 9:3).

It is almost impossible to grasp the brilliance of what Paul is saying here, and it makes a complete mockery of Agrippa's outburst, accusing Paul of thinking that he could make him a Christian as the result of a few minutes' work. As Paul quickly showed him, time or effort were immaterial. He would gladly have spent all that he had of both, if it would lead to the conversion of even one more sinner. He was driven by an impulsion to get through. In a book called *The Company of the Committed,* Elton Trueblood has suggested that most of the evangelistic similes Jesus used had this theme of penetration. He goes on: 'The purpose of salt is to penetrate the meat and thus preserve it. The function of light is to penetrate the darkness. The only use of keys is to penetrate the lock. Bread is worthless unless it penetrates the body. Water penetrates the hard crust of the earth. Leaven penetrates the dough to make it rise.' Does all of this say anything about your own evangelistic concern? In the New Testament, a Christian is a person under impulsion, someone who has a message to give and who is determined to get through to a world that so desperately needs what he has to say.

3. A man under invasion

The third reference to the word 'Christian' comes in one of Peter's letters. Writing to Christians under pressure, he warns them that they may well have to suffer for their faith and adds, 'However, if you suffer as a Christian, do not be ashamed, but praise God that you bear that name' (1 Peter 4:16). To say that a Christian is a man under invasion after saying that he is a man under impulsion may sound vaguely like a contradiction, but it is not. A Christian invades and is invaded; he attacks and is attacked. He is commanded to go into the world, and at the same time to prevent the world from getting into him.

No New Testament writer is more insistent than Peter on the point that a Christian is under invasion in this world. He warns them that they have to reckon with 'all kinds of trials' (1 Peter 1:6); he tells of situations where Christians may well 'suffer for doing good' (1 Peter 2:20); he says they may 'suffer for what is right' (1 Peter 3:14) and be 'insulted because of the name of Christ' (1 Peter 4:14); he tells his readers that 'Your enemy the devil prowls around like a roaring lion looking for someone to devour' (1 Peter 5:8); he prophesies the danger of 'false teachers among you' (2 Peter 2:1) and prepares his readers to face ridicule by those 'scoffing and following their own evil desires' (2 Peter 3:3); and he warns them to 'be on your guard so that you may not be carried away by the error of lawless men and fall from your secure position' (2 Peter 3:17). One has only to read those phrases together to see that this was one of Peter's major themes and concerns; and perhaps, on reflection, that is hardly surprising. After all, he would vividly remember Jesus saying to him, 'Simon, Simon, Satan has asked to sift you as wheat' (Luke 22:31). He would remember how he boasted to Jesus, 'Even if all fall away on account of you, I never will' (Matthew 26:33), only to be swept to the ground in shameful cowardice a few hours later. He would remember other attacks, too, by both civic and religious authorities. Peter knew what the inside of a prison cell looked like.

He knew the biting pain of being lashed by the three-pronged scourge, under which Paul had nearly died. Yes, Peter was qualified to write about the Christian being a man under invasion; but what are the lessons for us? Here are two.

Firstly, expect invasions as being usual.   Earlier in this chapter, Peter writes, 'Dear friends, do not be surprised at the painful trial you are suffering, as though something strange were happening to you' (1 Peter 4:12). A Christian may be surprised at the timing or direction of a spiritual attack upon him, but he should never be surprised by the *fact* that he is attacked. The devil may change his tactics, but never his principles. He thrives on attack. Paul tells us that every temptation that comes to us is 'common to man' (1 Corinthians 10:13). Those three words are just one in the Greek — *anthropinos* — which literally means 'of man', or 'human'. A Christian must expect these things. There is nothing strange about them. They are inevitable. They are part of the human scene. A phrase in Acts 14 bears this out exactly. Paul and Barnabas had been teaching new converts in Lystra, Iconium and Antioch, and in the course of what they said they encouraged them 'to remain true to the faith' (Acts 14:22). Well, of course, that is exactly what we should expect them to say in that kind of situation. But they went on to add this: 'We must go through many hardships to enter the kingdom of God' (Acts 14:22). Not 'we may', but 'we *must*'! There is no such thing as an easy Christianity. *If it is easy, it is not Christianity; if it is Christianity, it is not easy.* Living as we do in the alien environment of a godless world, there is no way in which we can escape being attacked. To recognize this is to build a barrier against depression and despair when the going gets tough. Especially if you are a young Christian, settle it in your mind here and now that the going *will* be tough, and that the closer you seek to follow Christ the closer you will come to the centre of the devil's target area. Expect invasions as being usual! *Secondly, accept them as being usable.* In *As You Like It,* Shakespeare makes the duke say,

> Sweet are the uses of adversity
> Which, like the toad, ugly and venomous,
> Wears yet a precious jewel in his head.

That is not the only place where Shakespeare captured a profound truth about life, but if we turn to the Bible instead of the bard we have this particular point on much better authority. In the sermon on the mount Jesus says, 'Blessed are you when people insult you, persecute you and falsely say all kinds of evil against you because of me. Rejoice and be glad, because great is your reward in heaven, for in the same way they persecuted the prophets who were before you' (Matthew 5:11–12).

Here is one picture of the Christian under invasion. He is being persecuted and reviled. All kinds of evil things are being said against him because of his stand as a Christian. What are we to do when that kind of thing happens to us? Jesus tells us that we are to use it as a means of helping us to contemplate and rejoice in the eternal glory and reward that will be ours in heaven, and as a means of confirming in our hearts that we are following in the footsteps of the great men of God who also suffered for Christ's sake. Only the Christian is able to do that! When the unbeliever gets hit or gets hurt his only responses are to hit back, to grin and bear it, or to grow bitter and depressed. But the Christian can actually take the most savage attack and use it as the theme for an anthem of praise to God.

James paints a very similar picture: 'Consider it pure joy, my brothers, whenever you face trials of many kinds, because you know that the testing of your faith develops perseverance. Perseverance must finish its work so that you may be mature and complete, not lacking anything' (James 1:2—4). Here again, notice that trials are to be seen as usable. They test a man's character. They help him to grow spiritual muscle. They develop and deepen the fibre of his personality. Without pressure, a Christian would grow feeble and flabby. Only as he faces up to life's problems and learns to overcome them will he grow to spiritual maturity. Happy the Christian who sees every trial as a means to that end!

Paul, too, says much the same sort of thing. When God showed him that his mysterious 'thorn in the flesh' was not going to be removed, he responded by saying, 'Therefore I will boast all the more gladly about my weaknesses, so that Christ's power may rest on me. That is why, for Christ's sake, I delight in weaknesses, in insults, in hardships, in persecutions, in difficulties. For when I am weak, then I am strong' (2 Corinthians 12:9—10). What Paul is saying is that these pressures and trials enabled him to recognize just how frail and helpless he was, *and that they did something else.* They forced him to stop trusting in his own power, ability, eloquence, enthusiasm or courage, and to trust instead in the all-sufficient grace of God made available to him in Christ. Here is a fascinating and sobering insight into the human heart. Given half a chance, we jump at every opportunity of proving that we can 'go it alone'. We are incurably proud of our own ability, and often it is only when we find our defences cracking and our resources dwindling that we turn to the Lord and call upon him. When the enemy's attacks do that, they do us a great service. They become usable. They open a gateway to the grace of God.

So in this passage Peter says, 'But rejoice that you participate in the sufferings of Christ, so that you may be overjoyed when his glory is revealed. If you are insulted because of the name of Christ, you are blessed, for the Spirit of glory and of God rests on you' (1 Peter 4:13—14). As with Jesus, James and Paul, Peter sees the Christian's suffering as being usable. He sees it as a means of reminding the Christian that just as he is sharing Christ's sufferings now, he will share Christ's glory in the world to come. What is more, to suffer as a Christian is to know the assurance of the Holy Spirit's presence in one's heart and the outworking of his power in one's life. That beats Shakespeare any day!

Expect attacks as being usual; accept them as being usable. That, in a nutshell, should be the Christian's philosophy as he faces the trials, temptations and pressures of living in today's evil world. Moreover, he should do so in the firm assurance that even the worst attack, the most violent persecution, the most sickening body-blow, the most subtle trial, only come to him under the sovereign hand of God, and can therefore be turned to his praise. As John Hercus puts it in *Pages from God's Casebook*, 'The great blows of God are designed to stand a man up, to awaken him from the dream-world of his tiny humanity and make him take his place as an "image of God", as a creature made in the likeness of God.'

In other words, they are designed to make a Christian *be* a Christian!

9.

'... As he is ...'
The 'impossible' truth

9.

'... As he is ...'
The 'impossible' truth

It was to be John 17 tonight — yet again! Our informal evening discussions on this chapter of Scripture had only been meant to last for a few nights, but somehow those sharing that delightful fortnight at the little Spanish resort of Palamos could not get away from it. Early in that night's session, somebody commented on the number of times the words 'glorify' or 'glorified' occurred in the chapter, so we began to pick them out. Verse 1, for instance, then verse 4 and verse 5. Next we came to verse 10, and I began to read out aloud these words spoken by the Lord Jesus to his Father in heaven about his followers on earth: 'All I have is yours, and all you have is mine. *And glory has come to me through them.*' Suddenly, a hush came over the room. Nobody spoke, nobody moved. It seemed for a few moments as if nobody breathed, either. Those few words had stunned us all. Their effect was literally breathtaking; I can sense it again even as I write. Here was Jesus saying that glory had come to him through the lives of believers, that in some mysterious, majestic way honour was actually brought to his name by everyday Christians. I forget how the discussion went from that moment on, but I do remember that it was a long time before we could move away from the shattering impact of that amazing revelation.

There are other verses in the Bible that have had the
same kind of effect on me. One is where Paul, speaking
of the Lord Jesus Christ, refers to 'the riches of his
glorious inheritance in the saints' (Ephesians 1:18).
That Christians have a glorious inheritance in Christ
I can at least partially grasp; but that he should have a
glorious inheritance in us leaves me utterly baffled.
Then there is John's marvellous prophecy that when
Jesus returns to the earth 'we shall be like him, for we
shall see him as he is' (1 John 3:2). A missionary was
once translating this passage with the help of a native
teacher. When they came to the words, 'We shall be
like him,' the native laid down his pen and said,
'No! I cannot write these words. It is too much. Let
us write, "We shall kiss his feet."' I know exactly
how he felt; were the words not in Scripture I could
not possibly believe them to be true.

But it is another statement in John's same letter
that is going to occupy our attention in this study, as
we continue to answer the question 'What in the world
is a Christian?' Here it is: 'Love is made complete
among us so that we will have confidence on the day of
judgement, because *in this world we are like him*'
(1 John 4:17). As I went through my Bible looking for
answers to the question that forms the title of our book,
I came to the reluctant conclusion that it would be
impossible to pass over this verse. I say 'reluctant'
deliberately, because frankly I would have done so if
I could — not because I did not believe it, but because
I could not understand how such a thing could be true.
I wrestled and prayed with these seven words for hours,
and more than once nearly laid them aside altogether.
But finally, I was drawn back to them and I believe that
there are truths here that even I can share with you as a
means of blessing and encouragement.

In the course of our study, we shall touch on the

whole verse, but let us begin by concentrating on these seven words: 'In this world we are like him.' What is your immediate reaction to a statement like that? Mine is to protest loudly, 'But it's not true. I am *not* like Jesus in this world. He was everything that I am not and I am everything that he was not. In every area I can think of, we are poles apart.' And is that kind of reaction not backed up by Scripture? Towards the end of his remarkable life, the apostle Paul admits, 'Not that I have already obtained all this, or have already been made perfect, but I press on . . .' (Philippians 3:12). Again, writing to the Christians at Corinth, he speaks of the process of sanctification like this: 'And we, who with unveiled faces all reflect the Lord's glory, are being transformed into his likeness with ever-increasing glory, which comes from the Lord, who is the Spirit' (2 Corinthians 3:18). Notice that Paul says that we are *'being transformed'*, not that the process is complete.

Knowing these statements as I did, it was perhaps hardly surprising that I found this verse in John's letter the most tantalizingly difficult I had ever sought to study. Yet as I prayed over it and sought the Holy Spirit's help, I came to the conclusion that it summarizes the whole five chapters of the letter, in the sense that it gathers together the three themes that occupy most of John's attention as he writes. Beyond any doubt, those themes are *love, assurance* and *fellowship*. To put it statistically, those three words are mentioned about sixty times in John's 105 verses, or more than once in every other verse in the whole letter. Bear that in mind as we just glance at the words again. *Love* is obviously the subject in the opening phrase: 'Love is made complete among us'; *assurance* is clearly the point of the second phrase: 'so that we will have confidence on the day of judgement'; and *fellowship* is at the heart of the final phrase: 'in this world we are like him'.

Now let us turn to our study of the texts in which John is speaking of three things.

1. Our covenant position

We begin with those memorable last words: 'In this world we are like him,' because there is a sense in which they form the key to the whole verse. As I have already hinted, we can only begin to unravel the meaning of these words when we understand that John is not for one moment suggesting that any Christian is of the same moral quality as Jesus. John was not making a point of comparison between the kind of life Jesus lived when he was on earth and the kind of life we Christians are living now. Anyone who compares himself with Jesus in those terms does so as the result of ignorance or insanity. John is not, then, suggesting that we are morally as good as Jesus, but he *is* saying something even more staggering — and that is that *God treats us as if we were!*

To appreciate how this can possibly be so, we need to get to grips with one of the greatest themes in the Bible, the doctrine of imputation. 'To impute' is a legal expression. It means to reckon, or to take into account. It is to assume and declare a person to be in a certain position as far as you are concerned, and then to deal with them on that basis. The American theologian A. A. Hodge says that to impute means 'to lay to one's charge as a just ground for legal procedure'. That may sound terribly dull, but it prepares the ground for us to understand one of the most fundamental and exciting lines of truth in the whole Bible, which tells us that three things are imputed in the spiritual world. We are

mainly concerned here with the third, but will glance
at the other two in passing.

Firstly, Adam's sin was imputed to mankind. Paul
puts it like this: '. . . Sin entered the world through
one man, and death through sin, and in this way death
came to all men, because all sinned' (Romans 5:12).
When Adam first sinned he brought the entire human
race into a state of sin and under the judgement of
God, because he *was* the human race and the federal
head of all his successors. As Paul adds, 'Through the
disobedience of the one man the many were made
sinners' (Romans 5:19). Even more concisely he tells
the Corinthians that 'In Adam all die' (1 Corinthians
15:22). In those four words you have positive proof of
the truth of imputation: the fact that all men die is
proof that they are 'in Adam', that they share the
result of his fall into sin.

Secondly, the sins of believers were imputed to Christ.
This is where theology becomes exciting! Speaking on
behalf of all Christians, Peter is able to say, '[Christ]
himself bore our sins in his body on the tree' (1 Peter
2:24). The phrase he uses here does not mean that
Christ bore our sins in the sense of carrying them away
(although that is also wonderfully true) but rather that
he actually bore or carried them *upon himself.*

As Paul puts it, 'God made him who had no sin to
be sin for us, so that in him we might become the
righteousness of God' (2 Corinthians 5:21). To use
yet another picture, our sins were charged to Christ's
account. He accepted accountability for them as if he
had been responsible for them. He agreed to pay the
penalty we had incurred. To quote Paul again, 'Christ
redeemed us from the curse of the law by becoming
a curse for us, for it is written: "Cursed is everyone
who is hanged on a tree"' (Galatians 3:13). We can
never truly understand the wonder of this, but let us

at least try to grasp the fringes of its meaning. A Christian's sin is not forgiven and removed because God set aside his justice in favour of his love, nor because God makes exceptions to his law that all sin must be punished with death. In the death of Christ the Christian's sin *was* punished, the full penalty of God's law *was* paid, his justice *was* totally satisfied. Our sin was imputed to Christ. In the words of the hymn-writer,

Because the sinless Saviour died,
My guilty soul is counted free;
For God, the Just, is satisfied
To look on him and pardon me!

Thirdly, the righteousness of Christ is imputed to believers. Not only is our guilt transferred to Christ, but all of his obedience and merit are credited to us. Paul not only says that 'Through the disobedience of the one man the many were made sinners,' he adds that 'Through the obedience of the one man the many will be made righteous' (Romans 5:19). This 'one man' who makes many righteous is, of course, the Lord Jesus Christ, and the point Paul is making is that Christ's righteousness is credited to the Christian. He brings the same amazing truth into his own testimony when he speaks of himself as 'not having a righteousness of my own that comes from the law, but that which is through faith in Christ — the righteousness that comes from God and is by faith' (Philippians 3:9).

This is what is meant by the imputation of Christ's righteousness to the Christian. But notice very carefully that just as our forgiveness does not mean that God has denied that we were ever guilty, so our being counted by God as righteous, and being dealt with by him on that basis, does not mean that God says we are righteous *in ourselves*. There is no ground for boasting here. In Louis Berkhof's words, 'The divine declaration is not to the effect that these sinners are righteous in themselves,

but that they are clothed with the perfect righteousness
of Jesus Christ. This righteousness wrought by Christ is
freely imputed to them ... and all to the glory of God.'

Now I have called this transference of our guilt to
Christ and of his righteousness to us 'our covenant
position'. Let me briefly explain this. The Bible teaches
that even before the world was made, God the Father
and God the Son entered into a covenant of grace to
bring about the salvation of all believers. There are
many references to this in the Old Testament. For
instance, we have, as it were, a snatch of conversation
in which God the Father speaks to the Lord Jesus and
says, 'You are my Son ... I will make the nations your
inheritance, the ends of the earth your possession'
(Psalm 2:7—8). This statement ties in with Paul's
amazing words that Christians were 'chosen in [Christ]
before the creation of the world' (Ephesians 1:4). Here
is the heart of the whole miraculous drama of man's
salvation. No words of man can adequately put it into
one brief statement, but let me attempt it like this.
Before the world began, God determined to redeem a
people unto himself, to put away their sin, and to
restore the broken relationship it caused. This was
expressed as a *covenant*, something that God decreed
would be done. In this covenant, Christ acts as the
Representative of all those to be saved. In their place
he meets all the moral demands of God's law and atones
for their sins by bearing the punishment that was due to
them.

To see even that flimsy outline of God's plan of
salvation is to get further than many Christians ever
do in understanding their position in Christ. Is it beginning to fit into place in your mind and heart? Because
you are in Christ, the moral demands of God's law can
no longer harass you, and the penal demands of God's
law can no longer threaten you. No wonder David cries

out, 'Blessed is he whose transgressions are forgiven,
whose sins are covered. Blessed is the man whose sin
the Lord does not count against him and in whose
spirit is no deceit' (Psalm 32:1—2). Blessed indeed!

Now what does all that teach us about the meaning
of John's phrase: 'In this world we are like him'? If
I had to reduce it to one word, I would use the word
accepted. On the basis of the covenant decreed by
God the Father, carried out by God the Son and applied
to our hearts by God the Holy Spirit, we have been
accepted, received, welcomed by God. As surely as
Christ's saving work was accepted by God the Father
as meeting the demands of the law and the terms of
the covenant, so we are accepted by him. To give an
expanded paraphrase of the words we are studying,
'Although we are still in this world, we are accepted
by God the Father just as Christ and his saving work
on our behalf are accepted.' Surely this is the real heart
of what John means when he says that 'Our *fellowship*
is with the Father and with his Son, Jesus Christ'
(1 John 1:3). This is our covenant position. Now let
us link this on to another part of the verse we are
studying, which tells us of another amazing truth
flowing from the fact of our salvation.

2. Our confident privilege

The phrase concerned here is this: '. . . we will have
confidence on the day of judgement'. We have already
seen that as Christians our covenant position is that
we have fellowship with the Father and with his Son,
Jesus Christ. We are saved and secure. In this second
phrase we are going to see something of the Bible's
teaching about our right to an *assurance* of these great
truths.

In the church's history, one of the great debating points in the realm of personal salvation has been the question of the relationship between salvation and assurance. Many ecclesiastical worthies have got very hot under their dog-collars arguing whether assurance was *part* of salvation (that is to say, of the essence of it) or whether it was something quite separate from it, though closely linked to it. Put in the form of questions, is it possible to have one (salvation) without the other (assurance)? Is it possible for a person to be saved and not to be sure of that fact? Must a person know that he is saved before his salvation can be real? Can we say that a person who has no assurance is not in fact saved?

You may never have given a great deal of thought to the matter — and if not, beware of giving immediate answers to those questions! Even great giants of the church have given vent to strange statements on the subject. John Calvin, for instance, contradicted himself more than once on the subject of salvation and assurance, and Martin Luther is on record as saying, 'He who hath not assurance spews faith out'! Perhaps he has changed his mind by now!

What is clear is that there is a great need for sound teaching on the subject. A lack of understanding about biblical assurance of salvation has become the father of a horde of ill-behaved children in the Christian church today. Too many Christians seem convinced about their doubts and doubtful about their convictions. The story is told of the building of a lighthouse on a bleak headland on the coast of America. After a great deal of work, the great day came for the opening of this brilliant new aid to navigation in the area — and with opening day came the thickest fog seen in those parts for many years. Two old Red Indians stood nearby as the opening ceremony was held, and when it was all over one turned to the other and said, 'Waste of money. Horns blow, bells ring, lights flash, but fog come in just the same'! When it comes to the doctrine of assurance, we may never have had so many horns blowing, bells ringing and lights flashing as we have in the church today — and perhaps we have never had so much fog.

Yet whereas so many Christians are confused on the matter, the Bible is clear. In the verse we are studying, for instance, John says, 'We will have confidence on the day of judgement.' He is so sure of what he is saying that he speaks of assurance not merely in terms of the here and now, but in terms of that day when God will 'judge men's secrets through Jesus Christ' (Romans 2:16).

But to answer that historical teaser. Is assurance *essential* to salvation? No! No! A thousand times no! Let me give you three reasons why this must be the case, and allow you to fill in the remaining 997!

Firstly, because the object of our faith is Christ, not any emotions or actions on our part, and the two are quite distinct. Imagine that you are on a train journey from London to Glasgow. After an hour or two you feel tired and decide to have a nap. A few minutes later you have lost all consciousness that you are on a train, but it does not affect the fact that you are! Your body is still on board the train and you are still being carried to your intended destination, regardless of your feelings and emotions. So it is the *fact* of trusting Christ that brings a person salvation, not his *feelings* about it.

Secondly, the Bible teaches that Christians are to 'be all the more eager to make your calling and election sure' (2 Peter 1:10). There is an obvious inference here that it is possible to behave in such a way, or to neglect the means of grace so seriously, that a Christian becomes unsure of his calling and election. It does not say that a Christian's calling or election can be forfeited — that would make nonsense of the terms — but a person can clearly lose the *sense* of his certainty.

Thirdly, we have the honest testimony of those of God's people, throughout the Old Testament, on into the New Testament, and right down the long years of the church's history, who have found themselves wrestling at times with doubts, fears and insecurity. Some of the greatest Christians have had their faith shaken to the very roots, but nobody assessing their lives seriously questions the reality of their salvation.

But having said all that we must add this: *a settled assurance of salvation is both possible and desirable.* It is the ideal, the biblical norm, what God intends. Paul's prayer for the Christians at Rome was this: 'May the God of hope fill you with all joy and peace as you trust in him, so that you may overflow with hope by the power of the Holy Spirit' (Romans 15:13). John goes so far as to say that this same kind of longing for his readers is one of the main reasons he wrote this first letter: 'I write these things to you who believe in the name of the Son of God so that you may know that you have eternal life' (1 John 5:13).

This, then, is the confident privilege God wants us to enjoy: a settled, balanced, calm assurance that we are right with God, not on the basis of anything we are in ourselves, nor on the basis of anything we have achieved, but because we are in Christ. Yet we must insert a word of warning here. There is a world of difference between assurance and presumption. It is idle for a man to boast, 'I am saved', unless he can prove it by his life. I remember a man who runs a series of boys' camps during the summer holidays recalling how one of the lads had once said to him, 'What you tell us confirms what we see.' What a significant statement! The boy had put one and one together and made sense!

The teaching corresponded with the lives of the camp leaders. This is always the biblical pattern. Creed and conduct should look alike. As James puts it, the Christian should be able to say, 'I will show you my faith by what I do' (James 2:19). A man's belief and behaviour should go hand in hand, and when Christian belief and Christian behaviour join together, they enable a person to join John in saying, 'We will have confidence on the day of judgement.'

So far, then, we have looked at what this verse in John's letter has to say about two of John's major themes — *fellowship* and *assurance*. His third theme is *love*, and comes out in the third section of our study.

3. Our constant priority

John's statement is this: 'Love is made complete among us,' and the first thing to notice is that he is obviously speaking of love as a developing moral quality of life. In the previous verse, he has spoken of God's love *to* us (he says that 'We know and rely on the love God has for us' — 1 John 4:16); now, he speaks of God's love at work *through* us, reflected and developed in our lives. There is a vitally important link here. Throughout this particular letter the Christian's assurance is linked with the moral qualities of his life, and the quality most often singled out is *love*. For instance, John says, '*We know* that we have passed from death to life, *because we love* our brothers' (1 John 3:14). Further on he adds, 'Dear children, let us not *love* with words or tongue but with actions and in truth. This then is how *we know* that we belong to the truth' (1 John 3: 18–19). Sometimes he puts his point the other way around: for example, 'Whoever does not love does not know God' (1 John 4:8). He illustrates the same truth a little later when he writes, 'If anyone says, "I love God," and yet hates his brother, he is a liar. For anyone who does not love his brother, whom he has seen, cannot love God, whom he has not seen' (1 John 4:20).

Notice how John hammers home his point both positively and negatively. Love is the distinguishing mark of the Christian. It is a kind of test. Not only can a man without love have no Spirit-given assurance of his relationship with God, he does not even have that relationship. To put a wide-angle lens on this for a moment, we will see something else, and that is that people who are not Christians will judge us at this very point. Jesus makes this clear when he says, 'All men will know that you are my disciples if you love one another' (John 13:35). This point is very effectively taken up by Dr Francis Schaeffer in his book *The Church at the end of the Twentieth Century*. In a chapter called 'The Mark of the Christian' he says this, 'Jesus gives the world a piece of litmus paper, a reasonable thermometer. There is a mark which, if it cannot be seen by the world, allows them to conclude, "This man is not a Christian." ' He does go on to admit that the world may be mistaken in its judgement, because although we are Christians we are still human, we make mistakes, we are capable of failing, we love imperfectly. But this in no way lessens the impact of what he is saying. Jesus has given the world a right to make a judgement about our Christian profession *on the basis of our love*. Our theological grasp, our organizing ability, our qualities of leadership, our eloquence, our loyalty to the church — these things are irrelevant in the world's eyes. Let me personalize this. The size of your church, the number of big evangelical names you can drop, the number of committees on which you sit, the number of offices you hold, your acceptability as a

speaker, the popularity of your music — these are irrelevant at this point. They are at best purely secondary
when it comes to the world making a judgement about
your spiritual standing, and when it comes to the
question of your influence in drawing men to Christ.
What the world sees and knows and recognizes and
needs is *love* — and it is on that basis that it makes its
response. *People will not come to love what you know
until they come to know that you love.*

All of this makes love our constant priority. When
Mother Teresa of Calcutta was in London on one
occasion receiving an award for her humanitarian work
in India she said, 'The biggest disease is not leprosy, or
tuberculosis, but rather the feeling of being unwanted,
uncared for, deserted by everybody.' People suffering
from that terrible disease are to be found not only on
the streets of Calcutta, but in the offices, factories,
shops, board rooms, schools, universities and homes of
our own country, and the only person capable of showing truly biblical love towards them is the Christian
living in touch with the Lord. We must therefore seek in
every way we can to be the kind of people who can
make a valid claim that 'God has poured out his love
into our hearts by the Holy Spirit, whom he has given
us' (Romans 5:5). To fail here is to fail totally in our
witness to the world, producing the kind of embittered
response captured in these very pointed words I once
found pinned to a school notice-board under the title
'Listen, Christian':

I was hungry,
And you formed a humanities club
And discussed my hunger.
Thank you.

I was imprisoned,
And you crept off quietly
To the chapel in your cellar
And prayed for my release.

I was naked,
And in your mind
You debated the morality of my appearance.

I was sick,
And you knelt and thanked God for your health.

I was homeless,
And you preached to me
Of the spiritual shelter of the love of God.

I was lonely,
And you left me alone to pray for me.

You seem so holy,
So close to God;
But I'm still very hungry,
And lonely,
And cold.

So where have your prayers gone?
What have they done?
What does it profit a man
To page through his book of prayers
When the rest of the world
Is crying for his help?

Some of those words may sound a little cynical, but there is greater pain in recognizing that they may come embarrassingly near to the truth. The Christian is not only called to *be* good, but to *do* good. Yet there is a

price to be paid. When Evangeline Booth, daughter of
the founder of the Salvation Army, was asked the secret
of her power, she replied, 'First, love; second, love, and
third, love. And if you ask me how to get it, I answer:
first, sacrifice; second, sacrifice, and third, sacrifice.'
Those uncompromising words take us straight to the
words of Jesus when he said, 'Greater love has no one
than this, that one lay down his life for his friends'
(John 15:13).

When Jesus spoke these words he was obviously
referring directly to his own impending death on the
cross. Today, they are almost always used in the context of war or the defence of law and order. Yet the
words clearly have another significance, which we can
gather from the statement that preceded them: 'My
command is this: Love each other as I have loved you'
(John 15:12). When we take the two statements together, we can see their total significance. For us today,
true love involves the sacrifice of self on behalf of
others. It means being willing to deny yourself, your
own pleasures, your own ambitions, anything that
centres on self, for the blessing and well-being and
benefit of others, even those who are your enemies.
In his book *The Royal Route to Heaven,* Alan Redpath
comments on this verse in the context of the Christian's
influence on the unconverted, and what he says is
deeply challenging: 'That is the principle upon which
you are called to live as a child of God in the light of
the cross; to lay down your life for your friends, to
forfeit things you may consider to be perfectly legitimate in order that your friends may find the way to
Jesus more easily.'

That, surely, is the supreme sacrifice. Without wishing in any way to be insensitive, I believe that the
sacrifice of *self* is more costly, more difficult even, than
the sacrifice of one's body. The sacrifice of dying

physically is, of course, unspeakable, one that is perhaps beyond our understanding. But there is a sense in which we are called upon as Christians to make an even greater sacrifice while we live: the sacrifice of everything to which self clings in order that others, even our enemies, might be blessed. Only as we are prepared to make that sacrifice will we properly reflect the One who 'though he was rich, yet for your sakes he became poor, so that you through his poverty might become rich' (2 Corinthians 8:9). We will never be able to match his love, but we are called to mirror it, and to count this a constant priority.

What in the world is a Christian? Someone in the covenant position of being accepted in Christ; someone who can have an assurance of this as a confident privilege; someone who is called upon as a constant priority to reflect the love of Christ by sacrificing self for the sake of others.

10.

'... Many other words ...'
Guidelines to godliness

10.

'... Many other words ...'
Guidelines to godliness

There is a story about a man in the United States found guilty of a serious offence and sentenced to ninety-nine years' imprisonment. In any circumstances the sentence would have been severe, but this particular man had an additional problem — he was eighty-seven at the time! When the sentence was announced, he looked despairingly at the judge and cried, 'But I will never be able to complete it all!' 'Never mind,' the judge replied kindly, 'Just go away and do as much as you can'!

To condense the Bible's answer to the question, 'What in the world is a Christian?' into less than two hundred pages presents a problem of the same dimensions and all we have been able to do in these brief studies is to uncover part of the total truth. Yet perhaps doing so has given us a starting-point for further work, deeper study and greater rewards as we explore God's Word in our own individual ways.

Acts 2 records what happened on the Day of Pentecost and includes a summary of Peter's sermon on that day. I have called it a summary, because it is obvious that not every word he spoke then is recorded. Indeed we are specifically told that he warned the people 'with *many other words*' (Acts 2:40). In the same way, the Bible has 'many other words' than those we have studied to answer our question. For instance, Christians are described as 'ambassadors' (2 Corinthians 5:20),

168

'believers' (1 Timothy 4:12), 'branches' (John 15:5) and 'aliens and strangers' (1 Peter 2:11) and each of these descriptions suggests fascinating avenues of truth.

In this study, however, we are going to take a brief look at six other definitions of a Christian, clustered together in one passage of Scripture. But before we do so, let me remind you of a principle that has run right through these studies and that is that all doctrine is meant to lead to moral action. Let me put it like this: all the Bible's words to describe a Christian are nouns, obviously; but they should all result in verbs, *naturally*! Each one of them suggests things we should be or not be, do or not do. Hold this carefully in mind as we turn in a moment to what we might call a 'polyphoto' album of a New Testament Christian. In each case, we are going to make just one point of application and, as it happens, it will always be in the negative. But, to continue the photographic metaphor, there is nothing wrong with that, because the only way to get a good positive is to begin with a good negative. Eight of the Ten Commandments are in the negative, but what a contribution they make to positive Christian living! 'You shall not murder' (Exodus 20:13) is negative, but it safeguards human life; 'You shall not commit adultery' (Exodus 20:14) is negative, but it safeguards marriage; 'You shall not steal' (Exodus 20:15) is negative, but it safeguards property — and so on. A good, strong negative prepares the way for a good, strong positive. With all of that in mind, let us turn to Paul's second letter to Timothy and note six final definitions of a Christian.

1. A Christian is a soldier — he must not get diverted

Here is the first of these definitions: 'No one serving as

a soldier gets involved in civilian affairs — he wants to please his commanding officer' (2 Timothy 2:4). We have already devoted a whole study to the Christian as a soldier, but this further word from Paul gives the opportunity to underline one point that is certainly not difficult to apply today. Too many of our churches are like battalions of the Territorial Army — full-time civilians but only part-time soldiers. They are the kind of Christians whose major concern is in furthering their own ends and interests rather than in seeking to have a single eye to the glory of God.

The story is told of a watchmaker who enrolled in one of the armies fighting in the American Civil War. At one stage the war got bogged down and there was a long lull in the fighting. Soon, a table in his tent was filled with watches, springs, wheels and all the other bits and pieces you would expect to find on a watchmaker's bench. More and more soldiers brought their watches to him for repair and soon he was engrossed in his trade. Suddenly, the war sprang to life again and his regiment was given the order to move. Everybody sprang immediately into action — except the watchmaker. Noticing this, another soldier burst into his tent and shouted, 'Get up from there. Haven't you heard the orders? We're moving!' 'But I can't,' the man replied, 'I've got all these watches to repair.' He had forgotten the real objective of his being there, which was not to repair watches, but to be a vital part of a fighting machine, ready and alert to obey every order of his superior officers.

In the same way, many Christians seem to have forgotten why they have been called into Christ's army. There is more to being a Christian than attending rallies and services, reading and praying, singing in a music group, handing out tracts or writing out cheques for missionary societies. *All of life* is meant to be seen as active Christian service — in business and at leisure, at work and at home, in public and in private. All of life is to be viewed as a responsibility to please the One who has called us to be his soldiers. Every part of the Christian's life should be stamped O.H.M.S. — On His Majesty's Service. This was what Horatius Bonar had in mind when he used these words to summarize one of his hymns:

So shall no part of day or night
From sacredness be free;
But all my life, in every step,
Be fellowship with thee.

It is so easy to take our eyes off life's real purpose and turn them to secondary issues. Like everyone else, a Christian is involved with business matters, material and financial issues, family life, leisure time, social and community involvement, and many other legitimate issues. But they should all be conducted under the umbrella of this one great principle: the Christian must seek to please the Commanding Officer of his life. Paul went so far as to say that his consuming concern was that 'Christ will be exalted in my body, *whether by life or by death*' (Philippians 1:20). Notice that last phrase! As far as Paul was concerned, things like business success, popularity, wealth, health or even life itself were secondary matters. Whether he lived or died was a matter of monumental irrelevance. All that mattered to him was that he brought glory to the name of his Saviour. In Vance Havner's words, 'We do not have to live; we have only to be faithful.' And from that one, all-pervading principle the Christian soldier must never be diverted.

2. A Christian is an athlete — he must not break the rules

Here is Paul's second definition of a Christian in this
passage: 'Similarly, if anyone competes as an athlete,
he does not receive the victor's crown unless he competes according to the rules' (2 Timothy 2:5). This is
by no means Paul's only use of a sporting metaphor.
In an earlier letter he tells Timothy that 'Physical train-
ing is of some value' (1 Timothy 4:8); he urges the
Corinthians, 'Run in such a way as to get the prize'
(1 Corinthians 9:24) and tells them, 'I do not run like
a man running aimlessly; I do not fight like a man
beating the air' (1 Corinthians 9:26). Later, as he
comes towards the end of his life, he tells Timothy,
'I have fought the good fight, I have finished the race'
(2 Timothy 4:7). Nor is Paul the only New Testament
author to use this kind of language. The writer to the
Hebrews urges his fellow Christians to 'run with perseverance the race marked out for us' (Hebrews 12:1).

Taking all these references together, they suggest
obvious lessons — determination, discipline, dedica-
tion and so on. Yet notice that none of these is the
point Paul is making in the verse before us. What he says
is that an athlete does not receive the winner's prize
unless he keeps the rules. What does he mean? The
picture itself is perfectly obvious. The athlete who
cuts across the corner of the running track or deliberately trips a threatening opponent would obviously
be disqualified. In some sports the rules seem cruelly
strict. The great American golfer Tom Weiskopf was
disqualified from the 1974 World Open Golf Cham-
pionship for the technical offence of failing to sign his
card at the end of a round. The point, then, is clear:
if an athlete is to win, the rules must be kept. But
what about the spiritual application?

This would not seem to be quite so clear and

straightforward, though we can begin by clearing two points out of the way. In the first place, nobody becomes a Christian by keeping rules, that is to say, by obeying God's law. Nothing could be plainer than the Bible's insistence that 'a man is not justified by observing the law' (Galatians 2:16). What is more, nobody remains a Christian by keeping God's law or by leading a particularly good moral life. A Christian is both saved and kept by the grace and power of God and in no way by his own effort or achievement. We can certainly be clear on these two points before we go any further.

The key to understanding what Paul is saying here is to see it in the context of Christian service. Elsewhere he speaks of receiving 'the crown of righteousness which the Lord, the righteous Judge, will award to me on that day — and not only to me, but also to all who have longed for his appearing' (2 Timothy 4:8). James uses similar language and says that after a Christian has been tested he will receive 'the crown of life that God has promised to those who love him' (James 1:12). In the same way, Peter tells the elders among the people to whom he writes that 'When the Chief Shepherd appears, you will receive the crown of glory that will never fade away' (1 Peter 5:4). The picture seems to be that while Christians will go to heaven, and in that sense enter into the fulness of eternal life, some Christians will be particularly honoured as the result of their lives, experience and service. That seems to be Paul's emphasis here.

There is, however, an important difference between the metaphor and the application. On the race-track, only one athlete can gain the winner's prize. But in the Christian race the crown will go to many — *provided they keep the rules*. But what are they? We are not in fact told in this passage, but in my view the

answer lies along the following lines. When Jesus was
asked which was the most important commandment
he replied as follows: 'The most important one is
this: "Hear, O Israel, the Lord our God, the Lord is
one. Love the Lord your God with all your heart and
with all your soul and with all your mind and with
all your strength.' The second is this: "Love your
neighbour as yourself." There is no commandment
greater than these' (Mark 12:29—31). In condensing
the whole moral law of God into these two phrases,
Jesus is saying that *the Christian's rules are the rules
of love.* The Christian is blessed and rewarded, not
when he performs his religious rituals as a formal
mechanical routine, but when his worship is a genuine
expression of his love to the Lord. Similarly, the
Christian service that God has pledged himself to
honour and reward is not that performed as a clinical
duty, or motivated by a vague humanitarianism, but
that done with Spirit-given love as its supreme motive.

For the Christian, the law of life is to be the law of
love. That may sound trite, but it is far from easy to
keep this law. Unless we are very careful we can find
ourselves doing the right things for the wrong reasons.
Self-examination here can be painful. *Why* do you go
to church, read the Bible, pray, give? *Why* do you take
part in other Christian activities? Is it in any measure
motivated by self, or the desire to promote your own
church, or youth organization, or other group? If so,
you are breaking the rules and will miss the reward.

3. A Christian is a farmer — he must not evade the· burden

Paul's third description of a Christian in this passage is
as follows: 'The hard-working farmer should be the first

to receive a share of the crops' (2 Timothy 2:6). The two things that stand out in this brief phrase are responsibility and reward. Let us look at each of them in turn.

Firstly, there is responsibility. Paul speaks of 'the hard-working farmer'. Some years ago, a friend of mine startled his congregation by suddenly announcing, 'I think I ought to warn you that I am about to use a four-letter word. It may offend some of you. In fact, some of you would do everything you could to avoid it. But I am afraid I must use it, and here it is . . .' The atmosphere was electric! People tried to shrink back in their seats and look either uninterested or aghast. 'The word', the preacher went on, 'is *work*.' Gasps of relief all around!

My friend had a point. For too many Christians today, work is as unsavoury as a swear-word, with the result that many churches are suffering from a terrible imbalance — too many shirkers and too few workers. I am often reminded of this when making a plane journey. A plane with say a hundred people on board has something like ninety passengers and ten crew. Now, of course, there is nothing wrong with that situation, but when we find the same statistical breakdown in a church, then something *is* wrong. Switching to Paul's illustration, he sees the Christian as a *hard-working farmer,* and having spent five years living on a farm I have come to the conclusion that he would have been hard-pressed to find a better picture.

The farmer knows no hours; the demands on his time must surely rival those on the time of a doctor. There is no hour of day or night when a farmer might not be called upon to do some urgent task, and he must never evade the burden. The task facing the church today is overwhelming, but, as ever, 'the workers are few' (Matthew 9:37). When a little boy was asked for his favourite part of the Bible he replied, 'The bit where everybody loafs and fishes'! I am afraid that that situation is all too prevalent today. What is your personal commitment to the task of evangelism, the ministry of your church, the spiritual needs of your neighbours? Dr G. Campbell Morgan once said, 'Any man or woman in the church who does not know what it is to share the travail that makes his kingdom come is dishonest and disloyal to Jesus Christ.' Whole-hearted commitment to the work of God's kingdom is our inescapable responsibility as Christians.

Secondly, there is reward. Paul says that the hard-working farmer 'should be the first to receive a share of the crops'. The immediate meaning seems to be that Paul was telling Timothy that he was entitled to an adequate financial reward from the people he was serving. As far as he was concerned, he had a clear mandate for saying this: 'In the same way, the Lord has commanded that those who preach the gospel should receive their living from the gospel' (1 Corinthians 9:14). Although he waived his own rights in this area and worked with his own hands to avoid certain local problems, he claimed divine authority for insisting that those involved in the ministry of God's Word should be properly paid. The point is an important one for every Christian, who should see to it that his financial support of Christian work keeps pace with inflation and ensures that those in full-time Christian service do not fall short of God's biblical norm.

Yet there is a wider, spiritual application to this. Paul says that the hard-working farmer should get the first share of the crops — and the Bible teaches that in God's economy *he does*. The man who works hard and loyally at the impulse of the Holy Spirit is given rewards far beyond those that can be counted, weighed

or banked. This follows from the unshakeable biblical
law that *God honours obedience.* In James's words,
'The man who looks intently into the perfect law that
gives freedom, and continues to do this, not forgetting
what he has heard, but doing it — he will be blessed in
what he does' (James 1:25). Even more succinctly,
God says, 'Those who honour me I will honour'
(1 Samuel 2:30). Here is a spiritual law, by which
God promises to honour and bless the person who
submits to him and serves him in selfless obedience.
As William Hendriksen comments on the verse we are
studying, 'Similarly, if Timothy (or any worker in
God's vineyard) exerts himself to the full in the per-
formance of his God-given spiritual task he, too, will
be the first to be rewarded. Not only will his own faith
be strengthened, his hope quickened, his love deepened
and the flame of his gift enlivened, so that he will be
blessed "in his doing" (James 1:25), but in addition
he will see in the lives of others (Romans 1:13; Philippians 1:22, 24) the beginnings of those glorious fruits
that are mentioned in Galatians 5:22—23.'

That is well put, but remember that it is only the
Christian who is willing to assume the burden who will
obtain the blessing. A barren life is often the product
of idle hands. A Christian is a farmer and he should not
evade the burden.

4. A Christian is a workman — he must not be careless

Here is the next definition of a Christian that Paul gives
us in this passage: 'Do your best to present yourself to
God as one approved, a workman who does not need to
be ashamed and who correctly handles the word of
truth' (2 Timothy 2:15). The point about hard work
and the reward that comes from it has been made in

the previous section of our study. Here, in likening the Christian to a workman, Paul goes on to touch on two quite different issues.

Firstly, he speaks about the workman's aim. He says he must present himself to God 'as one approved' and who 'does not need to be ashamed'. It may be that we can best understand these phrases by seeing the first as referring to the Christian's standing before God and the second to his standing before men. In any event, the particular work that Paul is about to mention is to be done in such a way that it meets with the approval of God and man alike. There is a lovely parallel of phrases elsewhere in Paul's writings, where he says that 'The kingdom of God is not a matter of eating and drinking, but of righteousness, peace and joy in the Holy Spirit, because anyone who serves Christ in this way is *pleasing to God and approved by men*' (Romans 14:17–18). This should be the aim of every Christian in his daily living and service.

But we must add a rider to that principle, and that is that where the two conflict, the Christian 'must obey God rather than men' (Acts 5:29). When a situation arises in which we cannot at one and the same time meet with both God's approval and man's, we are to forfeit the latter in order to ensure the former. Yet whenever we can, we are to do our utmost to win God's approval and man's acceptance. To be rejected or criticized by our fellow men does not automatically mean that we must be acting in the right way. This is the line taken by the heretical Jehovah's Witnesses. When I have met them on my own doorstep and rejected their blasphemous denial of the deity of Christ they have told me that my attitude helps to confirm their belief that they are true servants of God, because he promised his servants that they would be rejected! That kind of reasoning is nonsensical, of course. My neighbour would be very angry if I started hurling bricks through his windows — but his anger would hardly prove that I was doing God's will!

Our aim in all that we do must be firstly to have God's approval, and then to ensure that when our motives, methods and manner are honestly examined by right-minded men, we have no need to be ashamed.

Secondly, he speaks about the workman's actions. Paul mentions one in particular here: he says the Christian must be one who 'correctly handles the word of truth'. The root of the verb means 'to cut' or 'to cut through' or 'to cut across'. It is the kind of word we would use about ploughing a furrow in a field, or squaring off a particular piece of stone so that it will fit precisely into a building. In both cases, great care is needed to ensure that the thing is done accurately. Here, Paul is using it in writing to a man who had responsibility for teaching a group of believers the Word of God. In contrast, he refers later to Hymenaeus and Philetus who had, in teaching that the resurrection of the body had already taken place, 'wandered away from the truth' (2 Timothy 2:18). Paul's concern was that in all of his teaching Timothy should plough a straight furrow of biblical truth.

As a seven-year-old boy, I was evacuated from Guernsey just before the German soldiers landed at the beginning of World War II, and eventually went to live on a farm on the Isle of Islay in the Inner Hebrides, off the coast of Scotland. I was there for five years, during which time I found myself doing all kinds of farm work. On one occasion the farmer humoured me by letting me try my hand at ploughing. He manoeuvred the horse and plough into position at the edge of the field, planted me between the handles of the plough and stood back. My big moment had come! Eyes sparkling with anticipation, I flicked the reins, signalling the horse to start. The beast responded with a sickening lurch that almost tore my arms from their sockets! I clung to that plough as if it were my last stitch of clothing, but from the moment it moved it was completely out of my control. At a speed that would have won it the Derby by several lengths, the horse charged across the field, dragging plough and boy in its erratic wake, while the farmer stood convulsed with helpless laughter. There could also have been just the suspicion of a smile on the face of the horse!

The illustration is unforgettable as far as I am concerned. Just as a plough needs to be handled by someone physically equipped to make sure that it produces a straight furrow, so God's Word must be interpreted in a way that is honest and accurate. This would have particular relevance for Timothy, of course, in his position as a leader, but it is not difficult to apply its lesson more widely. The Bible is not a general basis for discussion, or a collection of ideas open to private interpretation and adaptation. It is the living Word of the living God, and if a person aspires to teach its meaning to others he should remember that he will need both inspiration and perspiration! It is not enough to throw around some general religious philosophy mixed in with a few random texts. Every Christian who seeks to teach the truth of Scripture to others should do his utmost to understand its meaning perfectly and to preach its truth precisely. He dare not be careless.

5. A Christian is a vessel — he must not get polluted

Here is Paul's next phrase in this passage in which he refers to Christians in such a variety of ways: 'In a large house there are articles not only of gold and silver, but also of wood and clay; some are for noble purposes and some for ignoble. If a man cleanses himself from the latter, he will be an instrument for noble purposes, made holy, useful to the Master and prepared to do any good work' (2 Timothy 2:20—22).

In the verses immediately beforehand, Paul pictures the church as 'God's solid foundation' (2 Timothy 2:19) or, as we might put it, a firmly founded building or house. Now, Paul moves his camera indoors and says that in a large house you would expect to find a great variety of goods, articles and utensils, some expensive and others inexpensive, depending on their purpose. The parallel today would be a collection ranging from a silver tea service to a plastic wastepaper basket. So, Paul infers, the same is true in the Christian church. It contains a bewildering variety of people, from the saintly to the spotty, some a joy to the heart and others a pain in the neck!

But having given us that picture, Paul forgets about the vessels and concentrates on the people they represent. As Donald Guthrie comments, 'The illustration in fact digresses in its application. The variety of vessels in the house is intended to show the variety of types in the church, but the application fastens on the people and the vessels are completely forgotten.' Yet Paul does aim in one clear direction: he calls for vessels that are clean and thus useful to their owner. We have seen parallels in earlier sections of this whole passage. Just as the Christian soldier is to aim at pleasing his Commanding Officer and the Christian workman is to seek the Lord's constant approval, so the Christian as a vessel or utensil must avoid pollution, in order to be fit for the Master's use. Of the many things that are capable of polluting a Christian's life and therefore affecting his usefulness in the Lord's service, two arise from this passage.

Firstly, there is wrong doctrine. Nothing is taught

more firmly or frequently in this letter of Paul's than
the value of sound doctrine and the dangers of false
teaching, and there seems to be an indirect reference
to the matter here. The Amplified Bible translates part
of the text by speaking of the man who 'separates
himself from contact with contaminating and corrupt-
ing influences' and we can be sure that the kind of
influences Paul had in mind would be those inherent
in the false teaching of Hymenaeus and Philetus, to
which we referred a little earlier. The Christian has a
constant responsibility not only to avoid false teaching but to avoid compromising association with false
teachers.

Of course this is easier said than done. In my own
ministry I find that I have to walk a constant tightrope
between being involved in the total work of the church
and not compromising with those who do not hold to
the basic truths of the gospel. 'Speaking the truth in
love' (Ephesians 4:15) is not as easy as speaking the
truth or speaking in love! I must leave you to work out
the implications in your own situation, with the warning
that it may sometimes be painful and difficult. Yet only
by keeping unpolluted by false doctrine and compromising association with false teachers will the Christian be 'prepared to do any good work'.

Secondly, there are wrong desires.   This comes across
in Paul's very next words: 'Flee the evil desires of
youth' (2 Timothy 2:22). In his comments on this
phrase, William Hendriksen suggests that these are
pleasure, power and possessions: pleasure in the sense
of an inordinate craving for the satisfaction of bodily
appetites such as food and sex; power in the sense of
the drive to be superior, to lord it over everybody else;
and possessions in the sense of a preoccupation with
material things. Be that as it may, we should bear in
mind that Timothy was about forty years old when

this letter was written, and Paul's concern was obviously that he should be on his guard against the things most likely to grip him at that age and at that stage of his ministry.

From all of this, the lesson is obvious: *know yourself*. Recognize your weaknesses, your danger spots, the things that let you down, and keep close to the Lord for his particular help in those areas. When I lived in Croydon one wall of my study was festooned with all kinds of paraphernalia, including a plaque of Achilles, which I picked up in Greece. Achilles was a legendary figure from Homer's *Iliad*. When he was a baby, and thought likely to die, his mother dipped him in the waters of the River Styx, since it was believed that no weapon could harm a body that had been covered by its waters. But in dipping the baby in the water, his mother held him by the heel, which remained uncovered by water. In later life, during a fierce battle outside the gates of Troy, an arrow from the bow of the god Apollo struck him in that one unprotected spot and Achilles died of the wound. Only a legend? Yes, but a legend with a lesson. That plaque is a constant reminder to me of my own weaknesses and of my constant need to ask the Lord to keep me free from those things that would so easily pollute my life, ruin my testimony and spoil my ministry. Beware of that Achilles' heel!

Finally, in this section, a Christian is a vessel, but he is not meant to be an empty one. The old proverb says that empty vessels make the most noise, and that is sometimes true in Christian circles. For instance, I once heard someone say that the present ecumenical debate reminded him of a public swimming pool — most of the noise came from the shallow end! That may well be true, because Christians (like others) sometimes make a noise when they are unsure of themselves. But we are not to be empty vessels. Paul goes on to tell Timothy to 'pursue righteousness, faith, love and peace, along with those who call on the Lord out of a pure heart' (2 Timothy 2:22). The best way to keep a vessel empty of what is polluted is to keep it full of what is pure. A room full of light can have no darkness. The surest way for a Christian to be unpolluted is for him to keep on being filled with the Holy Spirit.

6. A Christian is a servant — he must not assert himself

Paul's final description of a Christian in the passage we are studying comes in this phrase: 'And the Lord's servant must not quarrel; instead, he must be kind to everyone, able to teach, not resentful' (2 Timothy 2:24). The word 'servant' is often used in the New Testament to describe a Christian and some of the lessons to be drawn are very obvious. But as with our previous studies, let us begin with the immediate point that Paul is making. As we have already seen, Timothy was responsible for the welfare of a local fellowship of Christians, and what Paul is saying is that alongside the unflinching discipline, the firm declaration of the truth and the fearless rooting out of false doctrine and behaviour in the church there must also be kindness and gentleness and the complete absence of a quarrelsome, assertive spirit.

Now let us move straight from there to the wider application. Paul uses the fascinating phrase 'the Lord's servant' — and it *is* a fascinating one because it is one often used by the prophet Isaiah when speaking about the coming Messiah, the Lord Jesus Christ. Several sections between Isaiah 42:1 and Isaiah 53:12 are commonly known as 'Servant passages' for that very reason, and in them we are told that one of the distinctive characteristics of the Messiah would be his refusal to assert himself even when persecuted and provoked. Here is an example, and one of the most moving: 'He was oppressed and afflicted, yet he did not open his mouth; he was led like a lamb to the slaughter, and as a sheep before her shearers is silent, so he did not open his mouth' (Isaiah 53:7). Centuries later, Peter was to confirm that that prophecy had been fulfilled, and wrote, 'When they hurled their insults at him, he did not retaliate; when he suffered, he made no threats. Instead, he entrusted himself to him who judges justly' (1 Peter 2:23).

Yet Christ's behaviour was more than just the fulfilment of prophecy. As Peter himself tells us 'Christ suffered for you, leaving you an example, that you should follow in his steps' (1 Peter 2:21). The characteristic servant of the Lord is to be gentle, gracious, forgiving, courteous and understanding, *and not to assert himself.* When Paul, a little later in his letter, commands Timothy to 'correct, rebuke and encourage', he adds that he is to do so 'with great patience and careful instruction' (2 Timothy 4:2). What a tragedy it is that some Christians, while having a considerable grasp of biblical truth and a commendable zeal for evangelism, also display the sweet approachability of an ancient porcupine and the tenderness of a runaway bulldozer!

But we close our series of studies not on a point of detail but on one of principle. A Christian is 'the *Lord's* servant', and when all the finer points of theology have been debated, when all the scholars have had their say, when all the authorities have been consulted and all the translations compared, nothing remains more simple yet demanding than the fact that the Christian is called upon to live a life of utter obedience to all the revealed will of God, and thus reflect in his life the One who alone has the right to reign over him. It is only what a

Christian is *in the world* that ultimately counts for anything in the kingdom of God.

Some years ago, Dr D. J. Hiley was a Baptist minister in Bristol. His son chose the medical profession for his career and for a while used a room in his father's house as his surgery. Late one night, there was a ring at the front doorbell. The minister threw open an upstairs window and asked what the caller wanted. 'I want Dr Hiley,' came a voice from below. 'Yes,' the minister answered, 'I am Dr Hiley.' Back came the reply: 'But I don't want the one who preaches, I want the one who practises.'

The message, surely, is loud and clear.